Country Clubs are nice benefits for people who enjoy golf. They are a function of exclusivity, there most often is a fee to join, and many require an endorsement from an existing member.

So historically you have to have the resources to join, the character to be invited, and the time to enjoy its benefits.

So what in the world does a country club membership have to do with sales? Well for our organization it had a lot to do with it and it was wrong, so wrong.

Our organization's success was driven by a few high performers fourteen years ago. We were very successful but also very tired and were attempting to grow others to repeat our success. Well, doing and teaching are very different and we learned this the hard way.

We built a country club for salespeople that they could enjoy on the first day. We built it because it's where we wanted to work, where we wanted to be. We should have known better and we forgot we earned the right to build it. We just didn't understand the consequences of letting everybody in.

Now, I am not a big fan of exclusivity or, quite frankly, of golf. This is an analogy and the reason we brought in Lance Tyson to turn the tides.

We met and unpacked where we were to date and our struggles moving forward. He had no idea what we did or how we did it, but he did know sales and sales might have been the last thing we were doing.

The next few years were a roller coaster. The laggards hated the new process. They couldn't stand being asked to stand up in a room of peers and state a vision for their role. The newbies didn't know better and the owners knew they needed to pull this off.

We went from one of the worst performances in our industry to one of the highest performances in just five short years. Was it hard, yes! Did we lose people, yes! Was it worth it, no question about it!

The hardest and the best decision was to humbly say we didn't know what we were doing and then get out of Lance's way. We trusted him and he trusted us. In the end, he taught me and our company a lot and we taught him a lot as well.

Today, we don't have a country club atmosphere; we never wanted one but built one arrogantly. Now we simply have a group of people that care about each other and are high per-formers in their own right! We gave people dignity, self-respect, goals, and activities that would lead to results and tools to help them grow!

SCOTT MCGOHAN CEO, McGohan Brabender

Lance Tyson has made a profound and lasting impact on the world of sports business. Lance prepares for a session like no other, he has an uncanny ability to read the environment of a sales team during a session and adjust his content to ensure they get the most out of the day. You, as a manager, will see the benefits of Lance's methods weeks and months after he is gone. I have utilized Lance during my tenures in the NBA, the NFL, and now on the agency side of the business. There is absolutely no one better in the world of behavioral modification, sales training, management training, or developing scalable sales processes that produce world-class results. Proud of you, my friend, and I thank you for all that you have done for me.

TODD FLEMING Vice President and GM, Legends Global Sales

Lance Tyson delivers the right combination of content and real-life stories that are insightful and applicable. His straight, no chaser coaching style is impactful and will drive you to focus on the "pleasing outcome," not the "pleasing process."

NICOLE JETER WEST CMO, Legends

The approach that Lance and his team teaches has been and is grounded in years of experience and ability to work through multiple situational dynamics. Their approach is one that is incredibly versatile and adaptable to all levels of products and demands. We have always appreciated their ability to challenge our status quo of thinking and put our team members in a position where they have, at a minimum, a technique and mentality that increases our probability for success. As we approach selling, we feel it is all about finding the balance between the art and science of the approach. The great part about working with Lance is that his approach is founded in both and he has the ability to balance that important equation in the mind of our sales team members.

NIC BARLAGE President of Business Operations, Cleveland Cavaliers

Lance Tyson knows sales! He is a master at getting sellers to crush goals. In Selling is an Away Game, *he gives you real strategies that can make a real impact on your business, your people, and your sales! This is the sales stuff every manager and salesperson needs today. Powerful. Timely. A must read.*

SAM CAUCCI CEO, 1HUDDLE

Lance Tyson was one of the first sales trainers I had nearly fifteen years ago in my first job out of college and his methods not only continue to be relevant today, but have applicability in inside sales, sponsorship sales, and leadership training. Lance's unique perspective and style continue to influence how I approach business from my days as an individual contributor to a member of the leadership team. His words are fresh, relevant, and so VERY Lance! I can almost hear him reading them to me audibly.

MEKA W. MORRIS Senior Vice President of National Sales, Learfield

As is usually the case when working with Lance, he comes out of gate strong and then he pushes the gas pedal further to the floor. In this book Selling is an Away Game, *Lance's philosophy hits you right between the eyes and you either get it or you don't. I would recommend you get it! My personal sales philosophies, built over twenty-five years of selling, have been impacted significantly for the good. His work with my teams, using much of what you will find in this book, has transformed my people from mere visitors with a prospect to valued advisors, good listeners, and strategic thinkers. Lance's ability to challenge the norms, be direct and challenging with his feedback, and yet garner trust from my salespeople is unique in the industry.*

BROCK WARNER

Vice President of Client Strategies and Principal, Advent Results

Our relationship with Tyson Group is the most important complement to our leadership, sales, and service teams. Their trainers simulate the best sales atmosphere while expanding each team member's ability to become a high-level producer and establish a long career in our industry.

BOB SIVIK

Vice President of Ticket Sales and Service, Cleveland Browns

Having worked with Lance over the last decade I know the power of his message and how transformative it is for sales organizations. His blend of humor, passion, and real-life experiences bring to life the proven, repeatable behavior that he has captured and is able to instill. This book crystallizes what I have experienced time and again in his training sessions and now shares it to a larger audience.

JOSEPH ONDREJKO

Senior VP of Ticket Sales and Service, Indianapolis Colts

Starting at the age of twenty-three, during my first career opportunity with the Cleveland Cavaliers, I was fortunate enough to learn how to sell under Lance. As my career progressed at the Cavs and then taking roles with the New York Yankees and PGA tour, I made sure one of the first things I did was bring Lance in to work with our sales teams, as well as assist coaching our management team. Even though I've participated in more than 400 hours of Lance's sales and management training the past fifteen years, I've always been impressed with how well he has been able to evolve his approach and material. What I cherish the most is the mentor and friend Lance has become. Selling is an away game, *but training is a "people game" and no better person to learn from than Lance.*

TROY TUTT Head of Partnerships, TicketManager

Lance's techniques and exceptional sales framework have enabled us to more effectively harness the considerable talents of our sales associates and evolve our team to the next level. His proven approaches, valuable assessment tools, and customizable, relevant, and—most importantly—practical training tactics have enhanced our sales approaches and empowered our team to hone in on the best strategies. We've worked with Lance for several years now and each of his sessions delivers unique value. His direct style and ability to break down sales scenarios—and, when needed, sales people—really resonates with our team. He shares the core of this training in Selling is an Away Game, *which makes it a vital read for both new and seasoned sales professionals alike.*

JOHN CLARK

EVP of Sales and Operations, Fenway Sports Management

Lance is a one-of-a kind sales trainer and, for my money, the best sales trainer I've worked with in a pretty successful twenty-three-year sales career. His immersive style and positive in-your face and hands-on approach changes outcomes, defines teams, and leads to more consistent and reliable success. I have seen it change the outcome of a campaign, project, or, in some cases, a career. His book is a must read and will help any sales leader or sales person be better at what they do on every call, in every meeting, and on every pitch. Leads will become legitimate prospects, prospects will become clients, and clients will become your most-trusted customers for life!

JASON GONELLA Vice President of Premium Partnerships, Prudential Center and New Jersey Devils

As the founder of a branding company that is on the cusp of trends in the market, I'm constantly in search of ways to help aid our process and help our sales team perform. The principles in Lance's book cross the boundaries to other realms of business by discussing positioning, marketing, and how to close and compete in a complex world.

COLIN CROTTY President, Hyperquake

Sales is a combination of art and science, with both functions being vitally important to an individual's success. Lance's teachings incorporate both of these concepts, creating a unique sales system that is above and beyond others. I have worked with Lance quarterly for the last fifteen years and consistently continue to learn and install his theories including sales, service, negotiation, leadership, planning, and management.

NICK FRASCO Senior Director of Corporate Partnerships and Suite Sales, Cleveland Browns

Selling is an Away Game *is like its author, Lance Tyson; it's unique. Especially in making clear the critical nature that resiliency plays in being successful in sales. Best of all, it's practical, proven, and works for all kinds of selling. Every sales manager should read this book.*

ED EPPLEY Owner, The Eppley Group

One of the biggest challenges young entrepreneurs face when building their organization is creating a robust selling operation. Most organizations and executives I work with talk about the weakness of their sales operations. What many of them don't understand, and could learn in Lance Tyson's book Selling is an Away Game, *is that a large part of sales success is centered on developing a scalable and repeatable selling process. Lance is the thought leader in helping organizations and their sales teams develop a robust sales process, he has done this for countless organizations worldwide. Now he has captured that process here so every organization can benefit. If you struggle with sales or your sales team, look no further than* Selling is an Away Game.

VINCE LEWIS
Director, L. William Crotty Center for Entrepreneurial Leadership;
Fifth-Third Bank Entrepreneur-in-Residence;
University of Dayton, School of Business Administration

In this book, Lance demonstrates that selling is a logical process. When the process is followed, sales happen. The steps that he outlines take us through the thought process of a buyer. People do not want to be sold and Lance clearly demonstrates a process that causes a buyer to say "look what I bought."

SAM IORIO Partner, Dale Carnegie Leadership Institute
Southeastern Pennsylvania and Delaware

Lance has developed and refined a business process. It is the process of selling. Tyson teaches the blocking and tackling of selling then helps to align the organization around its success. After all, nothing happens until somebody sells something.

BILL HUTTER Founder and CEO, Sequent Inc.

Lance delivers. Period. As a sales and leadership trainer, he truly brings theory to practice, and more importantly, partners with leadership to deliver results. This book is more of the same and should be mandatory reading for anyone engaged in sales.

BRENT STEHLIK Operating Partner, RedBird Capital Partners

We have had the pleasure of working with Lance and Tyson Group for over eight years. I can say, without any hesitation, his training, coaching, and direct approach to the sales process has had an impact with our entire ticket sales and service team. Most importantly, his management training program has helped expand the professional growth within our ticket sales and service leadership team. Lance's passion, team-first attitude, and overall genuine empowering personality allow him to connect at a level with all members of our ticket sales and service team.

KEVIN J. DART Vice President of Ticket Sales and
Service and Operations, New York Yankees

SELLING

IS AN

AWAY GAME

SELLING
IS AN
AWAY
GAME

CLOSE BUSINESS AND COMPETE
IN A COMPLEX WORLD

LANCE TYSON

Advantage®

Published by Advantage, Charleston, South Carolina.
Member of Advantage Media Group.

ADVANTAGE is a registered trademark, and the Advantage colophon is a trademark of Advantage Media Group, Inc.

Printed in the United States of America.

10 9 8 7 6 5 4 3

ISBN: 978-1-59932-900-0
LCCN: 2018946368

Book design by Carly Blake.

This publication is designed to provide accurate and authoritative information in regard to the subject matter covered. It is sold with the understanding that the publisher is not engaged in rendering legal, accounting, or other professional services. If legal advice or other expert assistance is required, the services of a competent professional person should be sought.

Advantage Media Group is proud to be a part of the Tree Neutral® program. Tree Neutral offsets the number of trees consumed in the production and printing of this book by taking proactive steps such as planting trees in direct proportion to the number of trees used to print books. To learn more about Tree Neutral, please visit **www.treeneutral.com**.

Advantage Media Group is a publisher of business, self-improvement, and professional development books and online learning. We help entrepreneurs, business leaders, and professionals share their Stories, Passion, and Knowledge to help others Learn & Grow. Do you have a manuscript or book idea that you would like us to consider for publishing? Please visit **advantagefamily.com** or call **1.866.775.1696**.

To the six: Dad, you were right when you told me the world is my oyster; Mom, your strength in the face of adversity is my inspiration; Zachary, Jared, and Cooper, your strength and honor make you three my heroes; Lisa, my penguin, your love and faith in me is all I'll ever need.

TABLE OF CONTENTS

FOREWORD

I n 2003, I was the vice president of sales for the Cleveland Cavaliers. This was before LeBron James joined the team and selling season tickets was a daily grind. Despite the setbacks, we had a great team, process, and culture in place, and we were making progress. Though, the Cavs' new president, Len Komoroski, thought we could use a little help. Len had been with the Philadelphia Eagles prior to joining the Cavs and had instituted sales training. One day, very early in Len's tenure, he walked into my office and told me that every salesperson at the Cavs, including management, was about to begin a twelve-week sales training course, just as he had done with the Eagles' sales team. The courses ran on Thursday evenings from 6:00 to 9:00 p.m. and were mandatory.

Now, at that moment, I had a few thoughts running through my head. One was that I wasn't totally sure I needed to go through twelve weeks of sales training (though I certainly did). Secondly, I thought about how the team would react to working the already required 8:00 a.m. to 6:00 p.m. day followed by three hours of training once a week in the evenings. Lastly, I wondered who this trainer, Lance Tyson, was and how he was possibly going to hold this group's attention for thirty-six hours.

I recall, as we settled into the ballroom in the arena for the first session, I was a little unsettled. I was tasked with introducing Lance who, at the time, I didn't know. But knew I had to appear enthusiastic about this opportunity to the sales team. I also had not been through professional sales training of any kind up to that point regardless of the fact that I had accomplished eight years in the business and at the VP level. I wasn't sure what was going to be expected of me in front of my team.

Fast forward to the end of twelve weeks and several things happened. First, I learned more than I had ever learned before about the sales process and the skills and tools that needed to be acquired and practiced. Effort, energy, and personal skills are helpful, but alone do not get it done. Secondly, I learned that Lance was extremely talented at teaching and had a wealth of knowledge to offer. And lastly, I learned a strategy that I would use in every sales situation I found myself in from that point on.

This was the start of a long professional and personal relationship with Lance as he became the sales trainer for the Cavaliers for the rest of my tenure. I then moved to the Dallas Cowboys in 2011 to lead sales for the new stadium. After my move to Dallas, Lance and I created an outsourced sales execution firm called Legends that has provided sales services to over forty sports facility projects. Lance has trained each one of our sales professionals. In my opinion, no one but Lance has his unique combination of sales knowledge, energy, and teaching talent.

I'm pleased to say that Lance has captured the complex process that leads to closing sales in *Selling is an Away Game*. What you will find within these pages is a true handbook on how to lead sales conversations. He teaches you how to think from the buyer's perspective so you can travel through a sales path that leads to the best result. Lance offers short stories from his own personal selling experiences and from the many sales teams he has trained. If you combine Lance's thirty years of personal selling experience with the thousands of salespeople he has trained, you can be assured that he has heard and seen every situation you could imagine.

There are two very specific tactics that Lance details in his book that really stand out to me. Whether you are selling a product, an idea, or simply trying to get peers or your team on board with a new concept, these tactics are paramount in any situation and surround open-ended questions and objections. Lance taught me, and continues to teach our sales teams, how to communicate with who, what, when, where, and why questions. These words have become a common part of my vocabulary and have helped me not only in sales situations, but in overall relationship development. Lance also taught me to embrace objections. Once you learn that objections are necessary in order to close, that they are your friend, your mind-set around objections will immediately shift. In his book, Lance walks you through the very specific details of what to do with objections and how to use them to your advantage.

When Lance trains, the time flies by because you are learning so much. It's entertaining; he has great energy and a million stories and examples. He has found a way to capture that same essence into the pages of this book. You will laugh and be inspired all while learning a process that defines successful selling. When I was young in my career as a sales rep, I was thirsty for knowledge. I took on the idea of becoming self-taught by reading books and listening to tapes. Nowadays, I am often asked for book recommendations by young salespeople. Selling is an Away game is now at the top of my list. Thank you, Lance for taking your knowledge and teachings and sharing them for all to see. You have given those willing to invest in themselves all the necessary tools to go out and carry on highly skilled sales conversations.

Chad Estis

Executive Vice President, Business Operations

Dallas Cowboys Football Club

INTRODUCTION
Screw the Better Mousetrap

LANCE-ISM #72
"YOU CAN'T WIN IF YOU CAN'T SCORE. GAME ON!"

There's an old saying attributed to Ralph Waldo Emerson: "Build a better mousetrap and the world will beat a path to your door." First of all, I don't know who his PR manager was, but that's not even what good old Ralph said.[1] Not even close. Second, the concept that the best product will attract customers in droves is dead wrong.

The fact is, inventors have been coming up with all kinds of innovative ways to get rid of rodents over the centuries—metal traps, paper traps, glue traps, user-friendly traps, environmentally friendly traps, and, the ever-ironic, mouse-friendly trap. To this day, the U.S. Patent Office has issued more than 4,400 patents for mousetraps. Yet the winner in the marketplace remains that old-fashioned wooden

---

1   Emerson actually said: "If a man has good corn or wood or boards or pigs to sell, or can make better chairs or knives, crucibles or church organs than anybody else, you will find a broad, hard-beaten road to his house, though it be in the woods."

spring trap we've all seen in old *Tom and Jerry* cartoons. Those spring traps have been around since 1894, when inventor, William Hooker of Abingdon, Illinois, patented his version, and they're still the best-selling traps to this day.[2]

Did the Illinois native really invent the better mousetrap? Not really. Some are more humane. Others aren't as difficult to set. Some are less messy. But for every ten mousetraps sold, eight of them are those old-fashioned, cheap, spring-loaded, wooden mousetraps. At one time, somebody decided they would sell those spring traps as the standard for mousetraps, and they remain the standard to this day.

The lesson here is you don't necessarily have to build a better mousetrap; you have to do a better job selling your mousetrap. At the end of the day, a sale is about selling something that solves a buyer's problem or creates an opportunity. As long as the product being sold is efficient and effective, be it a mousetrap or CRM software, it has the potential to sell. To unlock that potential, you need a sales process. And to do a better job selling your mousetrap, you have to understand that there are a lot of new variables in selling. Social media and online information have changed the game. Now customers have more information than they used to, and not all of it is accurate. But the bedrock of sales is what it always has been: we are people selling to people.

> **You don't necessarily have to build a better mousetrap; you have to do a better job selling your mousetrap.**

That is exactly what makes the process so frustrating for people when it comes to business-to-business (B2B) sales—no matter how many times we try to synthesize it, we still find ourselves selling

---

2   Mary Bellis, "History of the Mousetrap," ThoughtCo., last modified June 20, 2017, https://www.thoughtco.com/history-of-the-mousetrap-1992152.

person to person. Most industries have been able to systemize every-thing, though it's primarily on the retail and distribution side. One would expect the same with B2B and business-to-customer (B2C) products. Yet every statistic says the opposite of that. For instance, Daniel Pink quoted a couple years ago in his book *To Sell is Human*, that while one in nine Americans make their living in sales, the other eight out of nine are involved in some kind of business development role.[3] That's more than any other time in our history.

Take for instance the sales teams out there in today's complex world. Despite the amount of marketing automation data that tells us they've actually cut their selling time in half, there are more sales-people interacting directly with customers than ever before. It's almost a two-to-one ratio. You would think with all the business intelligence, data, and information out there, there would be fewer salespeople. But I've been hearing that since 1995. Even with the invention of all this technology—the internet, email, marketing auto-mation—there are more salespeople now than there's ever been. You

Even with the invention of all this technology— the internet, email, marketing automation— there are more salespeople now than there's ever been.

know what that says? That actually says that certain sales are complex enough that you need to have a person involved to help you in the buying process.

The problem with selling today, as this book's title suggests, is that there's no home-field advantage. It's an away game, taking place in the buyer's mind. As the salesperson, you have to determine how much the potential buyer, or the prospect, knows or doesn't know. They actually might have a lot more information than you, or a

---

3   Daniel Pink, *To Sell is Human* (New York: Riverhead Books, 2013).

different version of information, so you've got to somehow get into their head and enable them to share, so you can help them ultimately weigh out whether the decision's right or not.

Sales has become complex because nobody has figured out how to make it simpler. If you go back to the late 1800s to John Patterson of the National Cash Register Company (NCR), he invented a new concept called a cash register. At the point of entry, instead of shop-keepers keeping their balances in a ledger, they now could take a customer's money, push certain buttons, and it would tell them how much money they had left over in addition to how much product they had left over. Brilliant, right?

But you have to think about the late 1800s. How the hell are you going to get the word out about a cash register? Nobody knows what a cash register is. You've got Mr. Olson on *Little House on the Prairie* operating the mercantile out of a cigar box and a ledger book.

Imagine NCR's sales rep riding into Walnut Grove, going up to Mr. Olson and saying, "Hey, Mr. Olson. Do you mind if I ask you how you manage your money?"

Mr. Olson pulls out a shotgun. "What the hell are you asking me that for? That's a personal question," says Mr. Olson.

Then the sales rep might say something like, "Hey, hold on. I've got this concept. If you're like most storekeepers, you probably spend hours a day balancing your books, making sure you're following up on the Ingalls, who are always late and always asking for credit. You're trying to figure out what you have: how much yarn, how many yards of wool, right? I actually have this machine that can save time and be more accurate."

Mr. Olson is intrigued, but skeptical. "What are you talking about? What machine?"

"Well, can I show you?" asks the sales rep.

So he would train Mr. Olson how to use it. He'd have it for a couple months, put it on consignment. This guy John Patterson came up with a four-or-five-step sales process, and that's how NCR sold their cash registers.

Let's face it. What's really changed in sales since then? Not much. Now we communicate over emails, LinkedIn, phones and text messages in our selling. We still have to go through the same steps. The process is just a little longer, and there's more information to combat what the salesperson or company is saying about the product or service.

If you think about it, the buying process is the sales process inverted. Why people buy is how you sell. That's never going to change. You still have to gain their attention, their interest, see if **If you think about it, the buying process is the sales process inverted.** they're going to be open to a suggestion, dialogue to see if they want it, and then you've got to close them. You've got to get them to say yes or no. Maybe is not acceptable. Nothing has changed.

And there's no shortcut, no way to cheat the sales process. Of course, we're not talking retail. Not that the Apple rep at the mall demonstrating the next incarnation of the iPhone to a customer isn't selling. But there's a huge difference between an unsolicited sale and a solicited sale. Even with my company Tyson Group, formerly known as PRSPX, 10 percent of our clients may come from word-of-mouth, or from hearing me speak at a conference, but 90 percent of our business is generated through solicited sales where we have to identify somebody, get their attention, and get their interest.

At the end of the day, sales is a science, just a series of yeses. "Yes, I'll talk to you. Yes, you can ask me questions. Yes, you can present to me an idea. Yes, you resolved my objection. Yes, I'll buy." It's an algorithm of questions, each followed by five or six yeses.

But sales is an art as well. Practiced at a high level, the profession combines creativity with a process for predictable selling. The goal of this book is not to help you build a better mousetrap, but to introduce a tried, tested, and proven process that will help you sell your goods or services with consistent success. It's a process that will benefit any high performer—from entrepreneur to sales professional to manager trying to boost team performance—and anyone for whom selling is a matter of life and death.

> **The goal of this book is not to help you build a better mousetrap, but to introduce a tried, tested, and proven process that will help you sell your goods or services with consistent success.**

I have been a sales professional, entrepreneur, and have trained other sales people since the 1980s. My experience includes selling vacuums door-to-door in college; leading the largest operation for Dale Carnegie Training outside Taiwan and Hong Kong; building Tyson Group as the go-to salesforce trainers of professional sports teams and insurance organizations; and training over one thousand sales executives and sales managers annually. A who's who of top sports franchises turn to Tyson Group to help their sales teams move to the next level, including:

- Fenway Sports Management

- Legends

- Turner Construction

- Topgolf

- Waggl

- Dallas Cowboys

- New York Yankees

- Cleveland Browns

- Hyperquake

- McGohan Brabender

- University of Notre Dame

- Advent Results

Even as I write this, we're working with the sales teams of about 60 percent of pro sports organizations. They come to us because we've proven able to rationally assess their sales operations and people, while helping them develop and implement a proven sales process.

In the following pages, I will lay that process out for you. You will learn the common denominator of successful sales people, how the six-step sales process resembles a visit to the doctor's office, and the keys to good negotiation and sales team leadership.

This process works, and no matter how talented you are as

You will learn the common denominator of successful sales people, how the six-step sales process resembles a visit to the doctor's office, and the keys to good negotiation and sales team leadership.

a sales professional, you need a sales process that works. I learned that early in my career, and no one's a better example of it than my old friend, Richard Slatowski, but we call him Slats (ironic that his nickname was Slats and he worked in a job at a flooring company). If you walked into a room, he'd be the guy you wanted to have a beer with, the guy who gets to know everybody in the room. He was great at the art side of sales.

At the time Slats started his career, I was doing regular sales training with the company he had joined. I said, "Hey Slats, we're doing a lot of sales training with these guys. You should ask to get involved."

He said, "I don't need any sales training. You know me. I got this."

A little later, in the 1990s, the economy started to dip a little bit. I asked him how things were going. He said, "Man, sales are really bad." He started to explain where he was struggling.

"You know Slats," I said, "winning rapport, being good at the art side of sales is only going to get you so far. That gets you in the door. Having a predictable sales process to yield a predictable result is a big part of it, too."

I believed that then and I believe it now. The best mousetrap doesn't always win. The best salesperson doesn't always win; the best salesperson with the best process does. That's how you compete. That's how you close.

After all, selling is an away game.

CHAPTER ONE
Attitude Adjustment

LANCE-ISM #104
"BE YOUR OWN ARCHITECT.
THE WORLD IS YOUR OYSTER."

oel Adams has what all successful sales professionals need: grit. I first met Joel when I was working on training with the San Diego Padres' office. He was a sales person on staff there, and according to Jarrod Dillon (VP of ticket sales at the San Diego Padres at the time), Joel was among their best and brightest. Well, as part of Tyson Group training, we do assessments of the sales staff's skills, and we'd rated Joel low on some of them. Needless to say, this didn't go over too well.

Jarrod came to me and said, "Lance, I don't know if I agree with some of the results. Your assessment scored Joel Adams low on some skills, but I'm not sure that's accurate. He's one of our best people."

For a little context, we essentially build a profile around a sales person's key performance indicators and major goal. We can measure

240 skill sets and numerous sales roles. Then we look at how fast the sales rep can run the forty.

We look at their skill sets and train on those where skill is low, building exercises that allow the sales person to perform at a higher level. Overall, the assessment we use measures a person's potential to do well. If the assessment scores them low but they are doing well, then it means the company is getting more out of them than expected, which is great. If the assessment scores them high and they aren't performing, then they probably have the ability to do better, and it's our job to figure out what is causing the discrepancy.

"You understand that skill set does not equate to success," I said. He tilted his head like a curious puppy. I continued. "You and I know plenty of people who are extremely skilled. It doesn't mean they're successful. Let me ask a few questions about Joel. Is Joel your top guy or maybe in your top three or top five?"

"Top three," he said.

"Does he come in really early and stay late?"

"Yeah. He's an absolute soldier. He does what it takes to get it done."

"Does Joel hate to lose more than he likes to win?"

Jarrod said, "Yes, he's probably the hardest worker here."

"What you're saying is he has a can-do attitude," I said. "He's a hard worker. Hard work, isn't a skill. A can-do attitude isn't a skill. It's a choice."

Not to say that Joel wasn't skilled, but what stood out to his boss was Joel's EQ, his Emotional Quotient, his attitude control. Angela Duckworth, calls it Grit in her book *Grit: The Power of Passion and Perseverance*. It goes by other names as well. In a 1940 address to life insurance agents, Albert E.N. Gray called it the common denominator of success. It's this: "The common denominator of success—the secret

of success of every man who has ever been successful—lies in the fact that he formed the habit of doing things that failures don't like to do."[4]

To illustrate Joel's grit, check this out: He finally gets his big promotion, his dream job. A decision-maker at the Cleveland Cavaliers says, "Alright. We'll take this kid. He's a good salesperson and wants to be in management." So the Cavaliers hire him to take over the inside sales team. Within three months of him getting hired, the Cavs bring LeBron James back from Miami. So now that LeBron is back, management determines that they need to reshape the sales team.

Imagine moving from coast to coast. You move from the West Coast to the north shore of Cleveland. Don't get me wrong; it's a beautiful city. But much of the year it's cold and dreary. You're finally in your dream job, and the Cleveland Cavaliers bring back LeBron James and Joel starts looking for another job. Over time, through sheer grit, Joel worked his way up to Director of Business Development for the Miami Dolphins. Then, during a routine checkup in the summer of 2016, doctors found a tumor in Joel's brain. Surgery to remove the tumor didn't happen right away though, because more bad news took precedence. Doctors found that Joel had Hodgkin's Lymphoma, a type of cancer that attacks the immune system.

After six rounds of chemotherapy, Joel was cancer free. But he still had the tumor. Another twenty-hour surgery and the tumor was gone.

From the time of his diagnosis and all throughout his chemo, Joel kept right on working. After the surgery, he was in the hospital for two or three days, and then he was back on the job. I saw him a few months after that, and he was already jumping into training.

---

4   Albert E.N. Gray, "The Common Denominator of Success" (speech, 1940), Amnesta, http://www.amnesta.net/mba/thecommondenominatorofsuccess-albertengray.pdf.

That's Joel. I would have expected him to do just what he's done. It's that kind of grit, that kind of endurance, persistence, and perseverance that sales people need to have. And I'd say that's why so many sports teams connect with my process, because at its heart is the kind of grit it takes to win championship games. I'm competitive by nature, so I understand the kind of challenges involved, the perseverance required to close business and compete in a complex world, but only if you have the right process. And I love me a good challenge.

THE POWER OF PROCESS

There's immense challenge in working with teams in really tough markets. When you sell sports, you're literally selling something nobody needs. You just don't sell sports to consumers. It's not just B2C: it's also B2B. You're selling a single ticket to a person for a single game, or selling a company on putting their name behind the brand, or affiliating their name with this organization or that arena. Only businesses can afford a suite for $100,000. You have sales teams that sell naming rights for $12 million a year to a stadium, or the advertising that goes along with it, which is a really complex sale involving a lot of moving parts. You're dealing with ad firms and CMOs of Fortune 500s, and it's a fluid process with a lot of negotiation.

But whether it's selling suites to Fortune 500s, closing multi-million dollar naming rights deals, or selling tickets to the masses, it really doesn't matter, because it is the exact same process. That's the crossover power of our process that has made Tyson

But whether it's selling suites to Fortune 500s, closing multi-million dollar naming rights deals, or selling tickets to the masses, it really doesn't matter, because it is the exact same process.

Group what it is today. Because what we do works, I've become close allies with a lot of the guys that are at the higher-up levels. As they've moved around, they have continually come back to me and said, "What you did at the Browns I want you to do at the Padres. What you did at the Cavs I want you to do at the Vegas Golden Knights. What you did here at San Diego I want you to do at Tampa Bay."

We believe so much in our process that we don't teach a thousand different things. We teach six to twelve things about a thousand different ways. Simple is genius. And simplicity comes down to a common denominator of grit that these particular clients can relate to.

Last time I was in Salt Lake, I was with insurance sales brokers working with them on sales. We plug the same offense and process into tech, insurance, or financial. It's easy for us. We have a really good name in sports, and it's a great story to tell because we're with the biggest brands in the world, including the Dallas Cowboys and the New York Yankees.

The reason why we have so many alliances in this arena is because we also coach all their executives. They run the same offense we've taught them how to run. Remember: sales training is a subset of sales management and sales leadership. When we come in, we're augmenting and accelerating because our specialty is sales management, coaching, and motivating salespeople.

We do this by taking a diagnostic approach to understanding the team and the gaps that need filling. By adhering to the following process, we're able to gain a deeper understanding of the sales team.

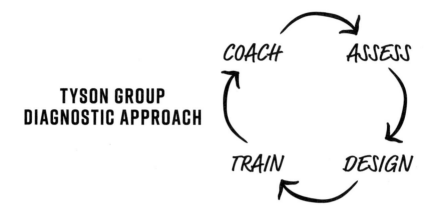

TYSON GROUP DIAGNOSTIC APPROACH

COACH · ASSESS · DESIGN · TRAIN

While writing this chapter, I was on the phone with Chad Estis, Executive VP of Business Operations for the Dallas Cowboys. He's had the same process since his days at the Cleveland Cavaliers. And every time he goes in, he installs that same sales management process, our predictable sales process. He plugs that in, and then he brings us in to work more with the people. Everybody that we do business with runs our sales process at some level: how to hire, train, lead, manage, and develop salespeople, while producing results.

In this book, I'm going to teach you a tested and proven sales process based on my decades as a salesperson and entrepreneur. It's a process designed with overcoming difficulties of today's marketplace in mind, and together we'll go step-by-step through the six major aspects of the sale. Each chapter is chock-full of practical and comprehensive strategies, real-world examples of sales in action, and a Highlights Reel section at the end to leave you with some comprehensive takeaways for successful selling. But for my process to work for you, you're going to have to dig down deep and develop the attitude that will lead you to better things.

> **For my process to work for you, you're going to have to dig down deep and develop the attitude that will lead you to better things.**

It's really about how you define and see yourself, that grit and persistence. Sales ain't easy. It's hard. You need to understand how attitude drives success, as it did for Joel, and how difficult it is to develop the right attitude. You also need to understand the difficult market environment sales professionals face today, regardless of attitude, so you can see for yourself why you need a predictable, proven sales process.

You can coach all day long for skills, and you can always pick up knowledge. But the piece Joel has, that attitude and grit, is something crucial someone has to pull from down inside themselves.

There's an exercise I like to do with management teams and salespeople in which they list attributes that would make their replacements successful. "If you had to hire somebody for your job and would get a bonus of 20 percent of your salary, what are things you would hire on?" I ask.

They will make a list of twenty or thirty things. But it comes down to three broad categories. At least 60 percent of success is based on attitude—things like grit, endurance, and perseverance. Another 20 percent to 30 percent revolves around skills like goal-setting and communication. The rest comes down to knowledge of basic theories and education.

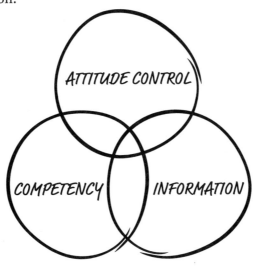

All of those things have varying levels of importance. But there's one key indicator of success. I like to put it this way: Successful people are concerned with pleasing outcomes. Unsuccessful people are concerned with a pleasing process. A successful person is totally focused on the result. An unsuccessful person is worried about how it feels doing it.

> **Successful people are concerned with pleasing outcomes. Unsuccessful people are concerned with a pleasing process.**

SEIZING OPPORTUNITY

A little bit of my own history may help illustrate how the common denominator for success plays out over time. I didn't like school, but I went to college anyway. Instead of asking my parents for money, I worked my way through. I sold Rainbow Vacuum cleaners door-to-door. I was a waiter. I worked at Pizza Hut and I was an RA.

In my senior year, six credits shy of my degree, I quit. The Berlin Wall had just come down, and in that moment I spotted an opportunity and started a business, Lancet Group International, exporting goods to Eastern Europe. I went out with my mom and bought my first suit, met with a professor at The Wharton School and sold him on helping me. Then, I tried to sell manufacturers around Philadelphia on the idea of letting me broker for them. I landed a grand total of one customer, PH2O Systems, which made water systems to test the epidermis of frogs. It was used in cancer research. They put me on retainer to sell their systems to universities in Eastern Europe, and eventually hired me as a salesperson. I never ended up selling goods overseas, but I was good at getting in the door, at building rapport and credibility.

That only got me so far, though. I realized what I really wanted was to be a public speaker, on my feet in front of people, and I remembered a friend had told me about Dale Carnegie and his book, *How to Win Friends and Influence People*. After reading it, I learned there was a Dale Carnegie office near my house in King of Prussia, Pennsylvania. I put on my only suit, marched down there, and introduced myself, astounding them because I sort of just walked right in.

But guess what? They hired me.

I started in January 1995, and I learned all about sales training. By the next year, I was married, and the lack of a degree stood in the way of my career advancement. Though I wasn't the most enthusiastic student, I went back and finished school.

In 1999, my mentor was Sam Iorio, the owner of several Dale Carnegie franchises. One day he asked me where I thought my career was going, what my goals were. I responded that I wanted to be a business owner like him.

So he set goals for me around sales, and, after a period of time, I hit those goals. Then he taught me how to start coaching sales people, even putting a few under my leadership. We set more goals and I grew sales and revenue. Sam then carved the entire operation into three different areas, leaving me responsible for greater Philadelphia. Sam continued to coach and mentor me, and as sales grew he added more responsibility to my plate. Ultimately, as I built up the territory, Sam allowed me to invest in the business as 25 percent owner. In fact, he sold me the same amount of equity he had sold to his own children. Sam knew how to run a business, how to grow people, and always did what he said he was going to do. He nurtured me as a businessperson and prepared me for future success. He also instilled in me the role of honor in all aspects of life.

In 2002, I had the opportunity to buy the Cleveland marketplace. Nine months after that, I bought Columbus. A year later, Cincinnati.

By early 2005, we had purchased Indianapolis and had become the largest Dale Carnegie operation in the world outside Taiwan.

In 2010, we pulled our infrastructure and sold our interest in the Dale Carnegie operations and formed PRSPX, now known as Tyson Group. Initially, there were two lines of business. One was a hybrid inside sales team where we took new college grads and had them work at setting B2B sales appointments. The other, sales training with a who's who in sports and entertaining. Realizing the need for this type of sales training and that my strengths fell in this area, in 2016 I restructured the company to focus solely on sales training.

I have become exactly what I set out to become, an entrepreneur. Only 4 percent of the businesses in the United States generate more than $1 million in annual revenue,[5] and I'm proud and humbled to say that my business is in that 4 percent. And now, I've become successful enough to be able to help others find success.

I wouldn't have made it if I hadn't been willing to do things I didn't want to do to get where I wanted to go. Whether I was going back to college to get ahead at Dale Carnegie, waiting tables to pay for school, or taking the risk of leaving Dale Carnegie, I was choosing a pleasing outcome over pleasing methods.

I was also working on other aspects of success, honing my skills as a salesperson, and gaining the knowledge I needed to advance. Those other aspects, though, were an outgrowth of my willingness to do what I had to in order to become a successful entrepreneur.

There's good news and bad news about the common denominator of success. The good news is people can develop a gritty attitude, often with their backs to the wall. The bad news is it's so hard to see

---

5   Adam D. Witty, *Lead the Field: How to Become an Authority and Dominate Your Competition* (Charleston: Advantage Media Group, 2016), 30.

the need to change ourselves sometimes that we go to great lengths to avoid it.

I have plenty of experience with that. I had been fifty pounds overweight for most of the past fifteen to twenty years. Not even seeing a dear friend and colleague lose a ton of weight and adopt a healthy lifestyle changed my attitude enough for me to shed some pounds myself. I didn't want to exercise or change my diet. I chose a pleasing method over pleasing results.

And then tragedy struck.

One of my closest childhood friends died. I was a pallbearer at his funeral, and I said to him, "Slats man, you got big, bud. You're heavy." After the funeral, I looked in a mirror at my mom's house.[6] Yep, I was as big as Slats. I knew something needed to change.

I decided then that I had to change and started getting to the gym, cutting carbs and shedding pounds, even working out at 4 a.m. when I had to. I didn't become a health nut or develop a new skill; I did it because I have three kids and I didn't want to die early. My pleasing result is sticking around and staying healthy. And it was worth changing my methods, and my attitude, to get that result.

The difficulty of changing, or even recognizing the need to change, applies to sales. As part of our training process, we do assessments like the one we did with the Padres early in Joel's career. Without fail, when someone has a low score, they'll say, "There's something wrong with the assessment."

My reply is, "Well, you didn't seem to have an issue when you scored high."

A big effort goes into getting someone to say: "Can I? Will I? Need to. Show me how."

---

6   She's an incredible woman. When I think about grit, I think about Joel, but I think of Mom, too. When Dad died, she was left with nothing. She is seventy-four years old, and she still works three days a week at Red Lobster as a server.

It's an effort you have to make. You must have that common denominator of results-driven grit for success. You have to persevere. The sales profession is so difficult. You get your ass kicked on a day-to-day basis. People say no to you nine times out of ten. People lie to you and act like your friend, then dodge your calls. If you don't have true sales grit like Joel Adams, at the end of the day, you're going to get your ass kicked. If you don't understand and adapt to today's marketplace, then that will kick your ass, too.

THE GAME HAS CHANGED

Sales has become an away game. It takes place in the mind of the buyer.

We have to get good at selling and creating rapport and connecting with people. In a rapidly changing marketplace,

Sales has become an away game. It takes place in the mind of the buyer.

we need the best odds to be able to do that. That requires both strategic and tactical proficiency. You need to win battles with tactics, and the war with strategy.

We need to be like my wife's hairstylist, Paul. One thing I learned was that if Paul moved, she would follow Paul. If Paul raised his prices, it wouldn't be an issue. If we moved, she would find a new Paul. There was this loyalty and connection that happens with somebody when you can give them your opinion and feedback, and everyone understands that there's a back and forth, a deeper rapport because both people have skin in the game.

It's a complex challenge to sell in today's marketplace, especially in B2B sales, but there's a simple solution, a process that levels the playing field for sales people through a step-by-step, replicable strategy that incorporates the tactics needed to win all the battles along the way.

Just how long are the odds for sales professionals? Let's take a quick survey of today's marketplace.

As I said, selling is an away game that takes place in the mind of the buyer. Those buyers have more information than they used to, which changes the dynamic between them and sales professionals. Once, a big part of what a sales person did was provide information. Now, thanks to the digital revolution, customers have a world of information at their fingertips.

The information isn't always good. It is estimated that 62 percent of organizations rely on marketing/prospect data that's 20-40 percent inaccurate and 94 percent of businesses suspect that their customer and prospect data is inaccurate.[7] But good or bad, the information is lodged in a customer's head. My inside sales manager once showed me a former Tyson Group employee's LinkedIn profile, in which he claimed he won Rookie of the Year at my company. Trouble is, we don't have a Rookie of the Year award. I sent him a note apologizing for missing the ceremony with a P.S. explaining that he might want to represent himself accurately.

I don't tell these stories to embarrass anyone, just to illustrate that there's plenty of bad data out there, even on LinkedIn. Inaccuracies, including the faulty information salespeople glean when they rely on the same online sources, ramp up the pressure on sales people. They mean a salesperson has to be asking the right questions at the right time in live conversation or through research. Sales people must take time throughout the sales process to take the temperature of prospects.

> **A salesperson has to be asking the right questions at the right time in live conversation or through research.**

---

7   Lauren Barber, "Data Decay: Is Your Data Rotten? [Infographic]," ZoomInfo, last modified January 5, 2018, http://blog.zoominfo.com/b2b-database-infographic/.

Not only has the role of sales professionals changed after meeting with a prospect, the time and effort it takes to get to that meeting has increased. Identifying an opportunity, pre-approach, and initial communication, are the most time-consuming parts of the sale process these days.

In B2B sales, it takes six to eight touches to get someone interested enough to even talk with you and another six to eight touches to get time on someone's calendar.[8] Those touches can come through LinkedIn, Twitter, even snail mail.

> **It takes six to eight touches to get someone interested enough to even talk with you and another six to eight touches to get time on someone's calendar.**

Since the 2008-09 Great Recession, price pressure has remained high, while the pace of technological change has been dizzying. Meanwhile, inherent objections like disinterest, disengagement, procrastination, and preoccupation, are as alive as they ever have been in buyers' minds, where sales professionals play their game.

Add the App Effect to other factors in the marketplace that have turned selling into an away game. When buying a product online, 92 percent of consumers spend time reading online reviews ahead of time and 40 percent of those consumers form an opinion by reading just 1-3 reviews. They insert their own confirmation biases and make quick decisions based on how well that product is customized for their own pre-determined needs.[9] It's changing how customers buy across the board. Customers want information at their fingertips. We can go as far as dating someone, finding

---

8   Fergal Glynn, "It Takes 6 to 8 Touches to Generate a Viable Sales Lead. Here's Why," Salesforce, last modified April 16, 2015, https://www.salesforce.com/blog/2015/04/takes-6-8-touches-generate-viable-sales-lead-heres-why-gp.html.

9   "How many reviews do you read before buying a product online?," Quora, accessed May 16, 2018, https://www.quora.com/How-many-reviews-do-you-read-before-buying-a-product-online.

out all kinds of details about them, without ever meeting them. They want products and solutions tailored to them, or customizable in the way a Fitbit is; though every Fitbit comes off the shelf, it feels tailored because it uses its owner's unique data.

I've had the pleasure of coaching and training Joel for years, and what's amazing about him, besides his resilience and grit, is that he's a guy that's looking to learn. That guy's looking to be coached.

92 percent of consumers spend time reading online reviews ahead of time and 40 percent of those consumers form an opinion by reading just 1-3 reviews. They insert their own confirmation biases and make quick decisions based on how well that product is customized for their own pre-determined needs.

To win the sales game, you need an attitude adjustment. You need to be willing to learn. You need endurance. You need drive. And you need grit. You need to harness your inner Joel.

I harness my inner Joel with the following mantra:

In the battle that goes on through life, I ask for a field that is fair, a chance that is equal to all in strife, the courage to do and to dare. If I should win, let it be by the code with strength and honor held high and if I should lose let me stand by the road and cheer as the winner goes by.

– Knute Rockne

I get to cheer for Joel.[10]

---

10   When I look at Joel and his fortitude, his grit, I think of my sons. Every night from the time they could talk, we would sit on the steps that lead to their bedroom and look each other in the eye and say "strength and honor" like a Roman legionnaire. Then, before they went to bed, we would say the above prayer. My only hope is they show the same grit Joel has demonstrated in his life.

Are you gritty enough to make it in today's marketplace? If so, this selling process is exactly what the doctor ordered.

- In the face of adversity, control your attitude.

- Grit takes no skill.

- Successful people form the habits of doing things unsuccessful people don't like to do.

CHAPTER TWO
Leveling the Playing Field

LANCE-ISM #144
"SIMPLE IS GENIUS."

For years, early in my career, I had done a lot of work with casinos. In doing some business with the Detroit Red Wings, I got to stay at Motor City Casino, which are both owned by members of the Ilitch family. I was talking to the general manager there, and he filled me in on how the casino was set up, and how a casino actually works.

A casino makes money at a higher percentage on some games than others. There's no secret to that. If you think about how Vegas is set up, or any casino for that matter, the game they really want you to play is slots, the one-armed bandit.

They want you to play the slot machines, because the odds are better for the house. If you go to a casino floor, you'll find they actually route you through multiple layers of slots. In the grand scheme of things, what are your odds, really, on slots? Who are the odds in favor of?

They're more in the house's favor. The barrier to entry for slot machines is low. You push a button and pull a lever. If you think about it, people like to play slots because it's not hard. You stick your card in, push a button, and pull a lever.

But if you made your way through the layers of slots, where do they start routing you? Where do the layers go? Well, if you went fifty feet up in the air, you'd see they start routing you to something a lot of people play: card games. The next game they want you to play is poker or blackjack, because the odds are still a little bit more in the favor of the house. And most people have been taught to play cards at some point, so there's a comfort level there.

The next game is roulette. This is where the odds start to tip a little less toward the house and more toward the player. You'll notice on the casino floor tour that there are a hell of a lot fewer roulette wheels than there are slot machines.

Then come the games that are furthest out, the hardest to access as a player: keno and craps. If you look at your odds, if you do any research, your odds as a player are some of the best with craps. Typically though, you have six to eight crap tables in a 24-hour casino. On average, probably three are being played at any one time. You have layers of what your lowest bet is. But if you pull up to a craps table and you start watching the game, you'll find it intimidating. Why is it intimidating? Well, you have ten to twelve people standing around the table, yelling and throwing things. There are distractions, and one person has the dice, but everybody's playing. They're high-fiving each other, and they're yelling about nine different bets out that seem very complex. But if you understand the game a little bit, they're not that complex.

Then you roll the dice and you say silly stuff like, "Mama needs a new pair of shoes." I remember I said that in front of my brother one time, and I won at craps. He said, "Mama? Who the hell calls Mom *Mama*?"

It's very distracting, kind of like today's marketplace, where you have social media and people's opinions and reviews and the like. But craps really isn't that hard, and you get better odds if you play it. If you keep your game simple, and you know the process, you can win.

In sales, we want to be playing craps rather than the slots. We don't have to be gamblers, but we do have to be odds players. Given all the challenges of today's marketplace, we need to learn a thing or two from the casinos. We need to even the odds, tip the scales in our favor … or should I say tip the *sales* in our favor.

> **If you keep your game simple, and you know the process, you can win.**

Think about the App Effect I mentioned in chapter 1. People buy an app because it's tailored to them or can be customized to meet their needs, or they perceive it as customized for them. The sales process needs to be tailored in similar fashion. The buyer is going to be concerned about how much things cost, whether their opinion will be taken into account, and if they even have the time to listen. And the buyer is going to be armed with more information than they would have been in the past, which is going to make them a lot more confident than they once were.

You need to have a strategy—a sales process—that takes into account all of those pieces of the buyer's mind-set. It has to be flexible enough that you can tailor it to individual clients, but sturdy enough that it can be scalable and repeatable. You have to have a predictable way to sell.

Once you are thinking strategically about the sales process, you incorporate the tactics and skills you will use throughout the process.

You're going to think in terms of: If this, then that. If I get someone's voicemail, what do I say? How do I deal with an objection about price? How do I give my Impact Statement? How do I present things in a logical fashion?

You're also going to be developing skills that apply in any process: things like verbal brevity, resolving objections, being able to facilitate, and selling over the phone versus selling in person. Remember, the sales process is simply the buying process in reverse.

These four parts—strategy, mind-set, tactics, and skills—work together to form the sales process.

Think about the steps you take when you buy something, a pair of sneakers, for instance. Something in your world gets your attention and you come to the conclusion: I need a new pair of sneakers. You start to go out and look, try a couple pairs on, go to the store, go to Amazon.com. In that process, you remove doubt, because you're actively looking. Then you start to consider it, lay it out and say, "Jeez, do I really need these? What pair do I need?" Ultimately, you buy a pair. That's a simple buying process.

In most sales, especially B2B sales, it's more complex. You take action to get somebody's attention. You need to qualify them to see if they would fit business parameters. You have to engage the prospect in some kind of request for their time, ask them a series of questions that are really for their benefit, and get the buyer in a scenario where you can present them with an idea in order to start creating an opportunity where one did not exist before. Then you present something that removes their doubt, and gets them saying, "This is a decent fit for me." Finally, you get into dialogue with them to remove any objection and close.

You're just inverting the buying process by taking every action that somebody would normally take when they buy something. That's the essence of the job. But to do that job well, you need a predictable process to get in alignment with what's in the buyer's mind.

It's not the kind of situation you will solve with the force of your personality, no matter how charismatic a salesperson you are. You need to have a repeatable system to address the complexities of sales in today's market.

You need a predictable process to get in alignment with what's in the buyer's mind.

Fortunately, there's a simple, six-step process that solves this complex problem. Each step addresses some aspect of the buyer's mind. In this chapter, I'm going to introduce the selling process and we will explore the tactics involved in each step in coming chapters.

The steps in the selling process are as follows:

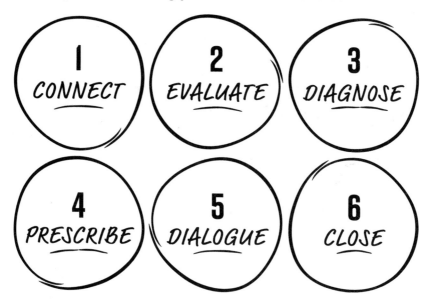

DO YOU KNOW YOUR DOCTOR IS SELLING YOU?

The sales process is like going to the doctor's office. Not because it's sometimes painful and uncomfortable, but because the steps of the sales process mirror the steps you go through when you visit the doctor's office.

Don't believe me? Think about it.

What's the first thing that happens when you walk into a doctor's office?

They ask you a series of questions before taking your insurance card and copay. In doing so, they're deciding if you're qualified to do business with them. At the same time, you're checking out the surroundings, the manner in which they treat you, and deciding if you want to do business with them. The **connect** step involves qualifying and evaluating, which you need to remember goes both ways.

In this step of the sales process, you're trying to get the buyer's attention by communicating things that are important to them, things that will engage and advance a conversation. This isn't just a self-serving step in which you're doing all the evaluating and saying, "Are they good enough to do business with us?" This is a point where the buyer is deciding whether they want to talk with you further.

To the buyer, it's no different than walking into a restaurant and asking, "Is this going to be good?" They're qualifying the restaurant as much as anything else.

> This isn't just a self-serving step in which you're doing all the evaluating and saying, "Are they good enough to do business with us?" This is a point where the buyer is deciding whether they want to talk with you further.

As a sales person, you might be connecting through social media. This step could include brief conversations. Connecting is a process in which you create an environment for asking and answering questions. There's candor and credibility. You can take this step through a conference call, an online conference using software such as GoToMeeting, or in person. In more complicated sales, it may take a face-to-face meeting to work the connect step effectively.

You're trying to generate interest from the buyer by asking the questions that will lead you to an understanding of where your product or service will benefit that buyer. You are trying to bring out the gap between the buyer's current situation and desired situation so that you can ultimately sell to the gap. You could be advancing an appointment schedule. You're introducing yourself, exchanging pleasantries, selling yourself, because at the end of the day, people buy from people. In this step, you're working to address the preoccupation in the buyer's mind to gain enough interest from them that they put aside their other issues long enough to give us some time and attention.

THE SOLUTION

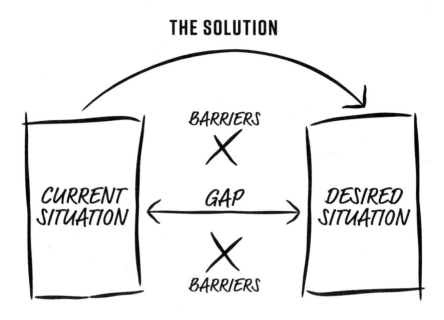

Keep this in mind as we think about the doctor's office.

After you have spent a little time in the waiting room of your doctor's office, you head back to another part of the office, where a nurse or nurse practitioner or doctor's assistant asks you questions about your health, weighs you, takes your temperature and blood pressure, maybe reviews your history. They're **evaluating** you. They're gathering information about your health based on age, weight, history, and all those other questions and the measurements they take. All while you're evaluating them, judging their thoroughness and bedside manner. The purpose of the connect step is to turn the disinterest in the buyer's mind into interest in you and the process.

In the doctor's office, the connecting process slides naturally into the process of **diagnosing** a patient's health issues. Once a nurse or doctor's assistant has connected and started the evaluation, they hand you off to the doctor, who will continue the process and work toward a diagnosis.

The doctor's manner, the questions he or she asks, the level to which they seem to be listening to a patient's questions and concerns, will all play into how a patient reacts to the doctor's diagnosis. In a sense, the patient is diagnosing the doctor's capacity to accurately gauge the patient's health issues. As with other steps in this process, the diagnosis cuts both ways. In sales, as you're going through the questioning process of evaluation, you're also starting to form your diagnosis.

In this step, you're telling stories and using examples. You're starting to firm up some of your suggestions and talking about your products or services. All of that is geared toward getting a read on the buyer's situation. You're adjusting the diagnosis based on the feedback you get from the buyer, while drilling down to make sure you're diagnosing the buyer's needs. Simultaneously, you're making the buyer a partner in this investigation. As with the evaluation, the diagnosis step is geared to turning disinterest in the buyer's mind into interest. It's also meant to start addressing a buyer's doubt by establishing your capabilities.

Once a doctor is sure of his or her diagnosis, they will **prescribe** something to address a health issue. They may say something along the lines of: "I'm going to give you Tylenol with codeine for that nasty sore throat. Stay away from beer and that John Deere while you're taking it."

In sales, as with the doctor, you prescribe a solution that addresses the diagnosis you've made. You're tailoring it as much as we can to the specific needs of the buyer. At this point, the buyer will want to know: What is it? How does it work? Who says so besides you? And can you prove it? You're going to give the buyer exactly the right amount of information, and no more, about the solution, to convince them that they're justified in buying from you. You're essentially trying to overcome the doubt in a buyer's mind.

All of this, though it is a step by step process, takes place in a fluid world. You may be able to cover all these steps in one meeting. All these steps could even be happening during a phone call. Or you could be making your prescription presentation in a third or fourth meeting after having had qualifying and evaluating and diagnosing meetings. It depends on the complexity of the sale. Your marketplace, your product, your vertical dictates the pace and complexity of a sale.

When my company sells training, for instance, it takes two meetings to get to the prescription. We have one meeting where we're qualifying and evaluating; another in which we come back and say, "Hey, based on what we heard, we're going to diagnose toward this a little bit. Let's set up another meeting so we can come back with a playbook and show you what we have for you."

We're trying to let the diagnosis take root before we prescribe a solution.

In some processes, an hour-long meeting can get to the point of presenting a prescription. In a doctor's office, this could all happen in forty-five minutes.

The point is that regardless of the time horizon or complexity of a sale, the process and steps remain the same. They're adaptable to any situation or customer, and at the same time constant.

But the deal isn't done once the prescription is given. Not in the doctor's office and not in sales. In the doctor's office, you don't just accept the prescription and start taking it. You're going to want to understand the implications, the cause/effect, what will happen if you don't accept the prescription, and what will happen if you do. Somewhere inside you, you may feel resistance to the prescription. You may want to put off taking it. The doctor's going to need to have a conversation, however brief, that addresses these issues. Or you just may not take the prescription.

Procrastination can be a powerful force in a buyer's mind. But it can be addressed in our next step: **dialogue**.

There's a dialogue in the doctor's office about the prescription. There's a back and forth about your understanding of it.

In sales, there has to be a scenario where you're asking the right questions to make sure the buyer understands what you're suggesting. You're talking with them to help them see how our product or service may help them now and in the future, asking questions like: "What do you like about this? What don't you like about this?"

You're trying to get them to a point where they're not saying, "Yeah, I understand," and then going away and doing nothing with what you've prescribed. You want to know if they see how they can use your prescription now and in the future, and determine their proclivity to buy.

In **dialogue**, you're helping them to clarify. You're showing them more evidence specific to them. You're empathizing with their answers and asking for more. Once you've made a compelling prescription, you need to know how you're doing and understand where the buyer is in the decision-making process. The best tool for this is the Trial Close. The buyer will give you one of three responses. They will be favorable, negative, or bring up buying concerns and resistance.

Inside the dialogue, you're discovering those objections. When you discover objections, you need to clarify the issue, find points of agreement, and create compelling reasons to move forward.

Again, think about the doctor's office: you've gone through connecting, diagnosis, prescription, and dialogue. Your objections have been addressed so that we won't put off putting the prescription into practice. Now it's time to **close**.

The close is no more or less than an agreement to move forward with the prescription. In sales terms, it's interchangeable with the commitment. This is what you've been working toward throughout the process and where you must overcome the last barrier in the buyer's mind—indecision.

That may require more dialogue, or negotiation. But throughout the entire sales process, you should have been gaining commitments toward mutually beneficial decisions. Those commitments you've built should have been eroding indecision as you head toward the final commitment, the close.

This process can be applied successfully to the most complex sale of capital equipment, or the simple sale of a pair of shoes, and everything in between. On some level, I've been working on sales processes since my days selling Rainbow Vacuums door-to-door as a college student, even if I didn't know it then.

One time during that period, I was trying to sell to a woman who owned two hair salons. This woman bet me she kept her house so clean that I wouldn't be able to pull any dirt off her floors. I made a bet with her.

"If I can pull dirt off your floor, would you buy a vacuum for each of your salons?"

She said, "If you can do that, I would."

"You can vacuum this spot with your vacuum, and then I'll vacuum it with a couple strokes of mine afterwards. If I pull some dirt up, no tricks, you'll buy two?"

"Absolutely," she said.

Well, I pulled dirt up because the technology was so good, and I sold her vacuum cleaners for her two salons.

My thinking then may not have been as sophisticated then as it is now, and I didn't know enough to know how to consistently make the process work. But I was still working within a process in which

I connected with her, qualified her, and where she qualified me. I evaluated and diagnosed what she needed. I prescribed a Rainbow Vacuum as her solution. We had a dialogue in which I addressed her objections by demonstrating the product. And finally, I had her commitment, and was able to close the deal.

Within this process, there's plenty of room for a salesperson's creativity and a customer's need for tailored solutions. At the same time, it provides a predictable, replicable path that can be applied across sales organizations large and small.

The process is a simple solution to the complex problem of sales. If you follow this strategy, you're on your way to competing and closing in a complex world.

- Don't be a gambler, be an odds player.

- For better odds, play craps, not slots.

- B2B sales are complex, but simple is genius.

- In sales, a predictable process yields a predictable result.

CHAPTER THREE
Fake News: Prospecting is Dead

LANCE-ISM #71
"DON'T CONFUSE ACTIVITY
WITH RESULTS."

L ately there's been a surge of advertising saying that traditional selling is dead, that prospecting is dead. I have two words for that: fake news. It's interesting that most of the stuff out there is from customer relation management (CRM) companies, or marketing automation companies, because they would like you to believe that you don't have to prospect anymore.

There's a multitude of reasons to believe prospecting is dead. Though social media avenues like LinkedIn make connections with C-level executives and decision makers much more possible, every salesperson in the universe is using it, thereby making it difficult to stand out. Also, office staff has little time on hand, meaning that you only have a window of about seven seconds to get past the gatekeepers.

Many salespeople end up as just another name in a missed call log, or forever lost in a collection of junk emails.

On top of that, we surveyed sales people in 67 training engagements between 2017 to 2018 and found that 40 percent of sales teams feel they do not have the right information before making a sales call. Did you know that poor quality data is costing your sales team at least 30 percent of revenues? Clean, accurate data is the difference for professionals seeking to streamline and clarify the front end of the sales cycle. Our studies show that sales reps are spending at least 32 percent of their time searching for missing data, then manually entering it into their CRM. Quality data is all about working smarter, preserving your resources, and accelerating your team's sales cycle. According to Salesforce.com, about 70 percent of CRM data "goes bad," or becomes obsolete, annually.

BAD DATA STATS

 of sales teams feel they do not have the right information before making a sales call

 of revenues are lost due to poor quality data

 of sales reps' time is spent searching for missing data

 of CRM data "goes bad," or becomes obsolete, annually

Bad data is bad for business. But no data, by not prospecting, is worse.

My meeting with Carl Asplundh proves that.

Carl was a C-level executive at Asplundh, the worldwide

company with the black and orange trucks you see just about everywhere cutting trees back from power lines. My meeting with him was one of the biggest I'd landed at that early point in my career with Dale Carnegie Training.

In my second meeting with him, I was ready to pitch our management training to him, and he, in turn, let me know via email that his lieutenant, Billy Anderson, would be there. In the email, it said clearly that his name was Billy. But I took a liberty. When I put the proposal together, I called him William Anderson.

As we sat down for our face-to-face, I passed around the proposal. We had good rapport right off the bat, exchanged some small talk and pleasantries. I felt good. It was one of those scenarios where you get a little momentum going. I handed out the agenda and discussion document. That's when Billy let me know his name wasn't William.

I could tell he'd done that many times. But it took the wind out of my sails. Especially since I was there to pitch them a large project helping their management team be more buttoned-up, take care of the little details, rise to the next level.

It brushed me back a step. I had screwed up Billy's name, and names are important. They were deciding whether to do business with me as much or more than I was qualifying them. I had to reestablish my credibility.

So many salespeople think that qualifying is something they do, when, in reality, the buyer is qualifying you and your actions. The credibility and trust you establish, the rapport you develop, your understanding of their business all play into whether they want to work with you. So do your appearance and manner of speaking.

THE SALES OUTCOME TRIANGLE

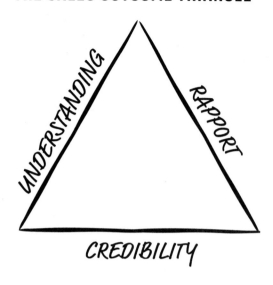

We can get lured into the Medusa's eye by the amount of information we can find. I can check out people who have visited my LinkedIn profile, find out how many employees they have, potential competitors, and other data points to help me start qualifying whether they might be someone I want to target. Studies have shown that 82 percent of executives feel their sales reps are challenged by the amount of time it takes to research prospects just to make the initial cold call.[11] To be more blunt, Google and LinkedIn have become the purgatory for inefficient sales reps.

We have to be careful, because Marketing Sherpas research shows that B2B data decays at a rate of 2.1 percent per month. This is an annualized rate of 22.5 percent.[12] I'm not saying to completely discount research. In fact, it's very important. I'm saying be careful.

---

11 Jeffrey M Luke, "82% of executives feel their sales reps are challenged by the amount of time it takes to research prospects," Jeffrey M Luke, last modified July 23, 2014, https://www.quora.com/How-many-reviews-do-you-read-before-buying-a-product-online.

12 "Database Decay Simulation: How Inbound Marketing Helps Overcome Database Decay," HubSpot, accessed May 16, 2018, https://www.quora.com/How-many-reviews-do-you-read-before-buying-a-product-online.

In selling, researching isn't our job, but it's part of what we do. It can tee-up an opportunity. We do some coaching with Fenway Sports Management, and at one point they were working on a large deal with a footwear apparel company. One of the junior salespeople had done their homework and won an appointment with the marketing and branding executive. For all intents and purposes, based on all research through social media, this executive had the title of someone who seemed to be the exact target to go after. However, once we got into a second meeting and the prospect became more comfortable as we had established more credibility and rapport, he was willing to include the actual decision maker in the buying process. Ironically enough, that person had a similar title to our first prospect. We would have never found this out through research alone.

Another example: I know a sports executive who has been president of an NBA team and an NHL team. With all the heavy lifting this person has to do—running marketing, sales, business operations, building a new stadium—sometimes social media isn't number one on their priority list. I know it took over nine months for that person to change their role on LinkedIn. If you were trying to do business with either of those teams, or that person individually, you'd be getting very conflicting information on LinkedIn as opposed to Googling them. Secondly, the individual who took that person's job would have the same title. Imagine trying to prospect that business and asking for someone who's no longer there. Would you lose credibility?

For salespeople, connecting involves gaining a prospect's attention by communicating briefly about things that interest the prospect. Research can help there. Just don't lose sight of the importance of back and forth communication in the connecting process.

Below is a brief overview of how we used to train our own Inside Sales Team on prospecting:

- It takes ten to fifteen phone calls to get a contact.

- It takes three to six contacts to get an appointment.

- If you call to confirm an appointment you risk losing it.

- It is crucial to send a calendar invite immediately upon setting the appointment.

- Phone appointments are at least 50 percent more likely to cancel/no show as opposed to a face-to-face meeting.

- The hardest part of the sales process is getting the first appointment.

- The most accurate list is the one you're actively calling into— data changes constantly.

- It is a waste of time to spend much time researching a company online—pick up the phone and call! Ask the gatekeeper questions.

- You're competing not just with other salespeople for the buyer's attention—you're competing with anything else they view as more important.

- You have seven seconds to get a decision maker's (DM) attention over the phone.

- Don't talk about the product, talk about how the product that relates to the DM's world is as alive as ever. If you're doing it wrong you may feel this is a useless endeavor.

When I had my call center, I remember fielding a question from a member of my inside sales team after she finished a call. She said,

"I just got off the phone with a guy who said he didn't have time to talk because he was in a meeting. That just doesn't make sense to me. I mean, why would you pick up the phone if you were in a meeting?"

Now, this situation was new to her and will probably be a new situation for any freshman sales rep. But I have seen situations where managers and directors were conducting one-on-one consultations or were leading a small group meeting and they stopped what they were doing to take a phone call.

Why would a decision maker stop their meeting to take a call only to tell the caller, "I don't have time to talk"?

The obvious reason why your prospects won't take your call is that they don't want to talk to you. It's a cover to politely hang up. As a sales rep, you have considerable control over these situations by how you set up your call prior to making it.

But what about the not-so-obvious reasons? Why would a decision maker pick up the phone when they don't have time to talk? Customer service managers do this all the time. Managers in post-sales support and service live in a reactive world. They expect their people to send unmanageable and irate customers their way. Or when the company's top customer has an emergency, they need to respond in the moment and manage the situation. They need to put aside what they are currently doing to deal with the customer crisis at hand.

Then there's the manager or supervisor who is conducting a one-on-one coaching session with a member of their team, but is expecting a call from his or her spouse regarding a family emergency. They will pick up the phone for that update, regardless of what they are doing in the moment.

These are just two examples. There are many more situations where a manager will pick up the phone even if they are engaged in an important activity.

So imagine how this manager or department head feels when they are in a meeting and expecting an irate customer, or bad news on a family member in a hospital, and instead they get you, a sales rep. And the only reason for your call is to talk about your product, your service, your company, or what you want.

Sales tip: see the world from the prospect's perspective. If you can see the world from your prospect's perspective, you will be in a better position to respond to their reactions when you interrupt their day.

Sales tip: see the world from the prospect's perspective.

GETTING PAST THE GATEKEEPER

I've done all types of real-time phone coaching with a variety of inside sales groups. Getting the gatekeeper to put a decision maker on the line is easy. Listening to the decision maker chew you out for a useless interruption with no value is a lot harder.

In my training sessions, on social media, and in consultations, I've had sales reps ask questions like, "How do I get past the gatekeeper? How do I get the president of the company on the phone?" Instead of asking these common questions, asking the following two questions will have a bigger impact on your perspective and your call results:

(**1**) Why am I calling this person?

(**2**) Am I flexible enough to see the world from the prospect's perspective?

The tactics and strategies that we review in our training programs and coaching sessions are extremely effective. However, nothing can compensate for the lack of a legitimate reason for the call in the first place.

When you are calling your customers and prospects, always know why you are calling. See the world from the prospect's perspective. And if you catch them in a meeting, they probably picked up the phone expecting the worst. Apologize for the intrusion, reschedule, and leave them something to smile about before sending them back to their meeting.

Remember, selling is an away game. It takes place in the mind of the prospect. Always leave your prospect or customer with something of value, and you'll be advantageously positioned for your next encounter with them.

DECISION MAKERS

On average, you should have three different decision makers within an account with whom you're cold calling. We define these decision makers as:

- Managers or Level 3
- VP/Directors or Level 2
- C-Suite or Level 1

In most B2B sales it takes two to three decision makers to influence a decision. This methodology for using cold calls to discover these decision makers is called spiderwebbing.

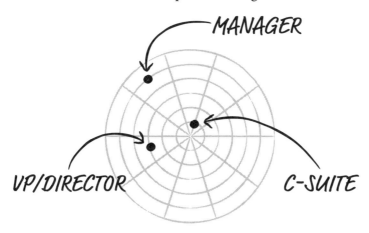

Although it is easiest to make contact with a Level 3, in order to shorten your sales process, it is important to meet with a Level 1 or 2 decision maker. Level 1 decision makers have more power and can make a decision quicker and will ultimately be the ones to close the deal. However, sometimes they are the hardest to get in front of. Level 2 decision makers may control the budget, but may lean on Level 3 to get their opinion.

The point is, people buy from people. And to do that, there needs to be communication.

The point is, people buy from people. And to do that, there needs to be communication.

Connecting is the first step toward doing that. It's the step where you overcome preoccupation in the mind of the buyer. You're going to do a much better job at connecting if you remember that qualifying and evaluating is a two-way street.

HIGHLIGHTS REEL

- Were you hired as a researcher or a salesperson?
- Using people's names personalizes everything.
- In prospecting, busywork is not profitable action.
- Too much data makes a salesperson slow.

CHAPTER FOUR

Connect: Finding That Common Ground

LANCE-ISM #12
"STOP SPRAYING AND PRAYING."

B y age twenty-five, I was a young professional making my way in the world. That's when a colleague of mine, Bill Chafee, told me to meet with some guy named Doug Moran.

I respected Bill. He was an elder statesman, a really good salesperson.

"Who's Doug?" I asked.

"He's my financial advisor."

"Why should I meet with him?" I asked. Did I mention I was twenty-five?

"Well, he's the man," said Bill. "He's going to set you straight for your future."

So I took my colleague's advice and met with Doug. He had this beautiful Merrill Lynch office in Wayne, Pennsylvania. It was one of those offices that dripped mahogany, really well done. I felt like I was in a Harvard library.

Doug asked me to sit down. "Lance, do you know why you're here?"

"Bill told me I should meet with you, that you were the man."

Doug laughed. "You're here because Bill Chafee told me you're an up-and-coming business person, and you might want to start thinking about your financial future."

I just kind of stared blankly. "Listen, I'm pretty young. I'm just starting out. I haven't given much thought about the end yet."

He smiled and picked up an egg off his desk. It was literally an egg. He said, "Do you know what this is?"

I looked at him. "Yeah. It's an egg."

"Do you know what this egg represents?"

"I have no clue, Doug."

"This represents your nest egg," he said. "Do you know what a nest egg is?"

"Yeah. It's what I would use to retire."

"That's right," he said. "Now, here's the deal, Lance. Over time, over your life, you're going to have a lot of people that influence, or hold, or carry, or do things with your nest egg to help it grow. You'll do things. Your 401(k) will do things, insurance. All kinds of things, people, and institutions will affect this egg. Do you know what's really important about this nest egg?"

He totally had my attention by that point. "No. What?"

"You've got to make sure whoever is handling your nest egg, at any one time, they're being really careful with it, and that they don't …" and from about shoulder height he dropped the egg on his desk where it cracked open and oozed.

I popped up. I looked at his beautiful desk, and I noticed he had laid some paper around to protect the surface.

Then he pulled out another egg. "Lance, do you know what this is?"

"It's a nest egg."

"That's right," he said. "What does this nest egg represent?"

"My financial future."

"That's really good. Lance, what's important about this nest egg?"

He had me. "It's important that people handle it with care."

"And what will happen to your nest egg over time?"

"Well, somebody's going to drop it. It's going to fall."

"Good. You're really thinking now."

Then he took the egg, and he dropped it on his desk in the same spot. It didn't break.

He picked it up. "Do you know what the difference between this egg is and the first one?"

"That one's hard-boiled."

"That's right. You've got to make sure, whatever you do with your nest egg, it's protected at all times. Whoever uses it, whoever's going to grow it, whoever's going to invest it, make sure it's protected. That's what we're here to talk about, for now and the future."

What Doug understood was that, at the end of the day, every single close is reliant upon a salesperson's ability to connect. At its heart, sales is about creating artificial momentum. Once you've mined that perfect prospect, your next task is to find common ground, to build credibility, to extract interest and create momentum where none existed. To do this, you need to see the sale through the buyer's perspective. If you want to sell John Brown what John Brown buys, you need to see the world through John Brown's eyes. You need to connect with the buyer and get them to

If you want to sell John Brown what John Brown buys, you need to see the world through John Brown's eyes.

overcome their preoccupation, because 95 percent of prospects see sales calls as an interruption.

Even as you are pitching, a prospect is asking themselves a series of qualifying questions about you: Is this salesperson credible? Do I have a rapport with him or her? Do I even want to deal with this person another second?

In fact, the first seven seconds are the most critical to get their attention. If you survive, you have the next sixty seconds to win their interest. And the first thing you're selling them isn't your product or service, but time on their calendar.

Most salespeople don't think that way. Most of the time they resort to using blunt force trauma. They smile, dial, use the trial, and go the extra mile!

That's why most salespeople suck. They don't think.

The ultimate goal is to engage a buyer in some kind of conversation, to get them to acknowledge that you are a person worth listening to and, hopefully, worth doing business with.

Remember, sales is a just a series of yeses. And those yeses begin through three key components: Sales Starters, Impact Statements, and Why Speak Statements.

The ultimate goal is to engage a buyer in some kind of conversation, to get them to acknowledge that you are a person worth listening to, and hopefully, worth doing business with.

THE SALES STARTER

The Sales Starter or Attention Getter is an opener. It hinges on the ability to gain favorable attention. To do this, you may compliment a prospect, ask questions, refer, educate, share information, or startle.

Getting a two-way conversation going is crucial, and questions are a great way to do it. Let's talk about Sales Starters. One time I was with one of my new hires, Ellen Valudes, at a meeting with a VP at Comcast. Sometimes pleasantries can take over a meeting, but Ellen is very gregarious and powerful communicator and I had coached her on that earlier.

As she was looking for her opportunity to bridge out of the pleasantries she said, "Did you know your sales people are stealing from you?"

I looked over at her, jaw wide open, not knowing what to say.

With a pregnant pause, she continued. "Every time they go into a sales call without a plan and a process, they steal time from the prospect, and from Comcast."

Ellen had both me and the VP at *hello*.

She went on: "Our meeting today is going to focus on ideas of how Comcast sales employees can leverage a predictable process to grow sales."

Having the right Sales Starter and Impact Statement can create a great opening. Contrary to popular belief, there is no skill in closing; it's all about a great opening.

One of the things the Miami Dolphins and Cleveland Browns do when they're meeting a potential partner in person is ask a question pertaining to time. They might say, "How much time is too much to talk today?" And the prospect may say, "Jeez, I've got about

> **Contrary to the popular belief, there is no skill in closing; it's all about a great opening.**

thirty minutes." Right there, the prospect gets a sense that this is going to be a two-way conversation and that their time will be respected.

In fact, the Miami Dolphins and Cleveland Browns, in particular, train their people exceptionally well at B2C and B2B conversations. A lot of salespeople confuse pleasantries with actually being the sales process. Ironically pleasantries—"How was your drive in? How is the weather? Where are you from?"—are not really part of the sales process. They are actually expected conversation in some places in the world. In other places in the world, it's very uncomfortable, especially in Asia.

We use Sales Starters like a question bearing on time (QBOT) in a layered attack. So if I ask a prospect, "How much time is too much time today?" they feel like

1. they have control of the meeting;

2. it's their time, so it's tailored; and

3. it's a Trial Close and they're telling me how I should facilitate the meeting and the allotment of resources I get.

Another Sales Starter is to open a conversation with a compliment. But if you use a compliment, don't be obvious or sound like a used car salesperson.

I once had a voicemail from a rep from Foursquare, the search and discovery app company. In the message, he said, "Lance, I notice you just published on LinkedIn about how to open a sales call and I see our values are aligned. Two of the things you mentioned are things we're coached on. I might have some ideas for you."

I qualified him on the fact that he had done some homework. As we got on the phone, he probably qualified me on a few things.

Educating someone can be a strong sales starter as well.

The Dallas Cowboys might call an organization that's thinking of doing corporate hospitality at AT&T Stadium and start off with, "Our clients tell us that saying thank you to good employees, customers, and prospects through hospitality has resulted in a higher retention rate and x return."

Let's go back to Doug's tactic to overcome my preoccupation of being young and thinking the meeting was a waste of time. His goal was to sell me Merrill Lynch's financial services. He could have gone the education route and said: "We're the largest financial planning organization in the world."

Well, that may be true, but it's hard to prove. A statement like that could potentially cause doubt. If instead he said something like: "We serve clients in thirty-six different countries and fourteen different languages." That's actually stronger. It's believable because it's specific and provable.

But why just throw that fact out there? What does it mean? Well, it means that he'll be able to service someone who has various locations around the world. For the education tactic to be effective, the salesperson has to be able to give a fact and tie a benefit to it.

Yet that's not what Doug did. He read me as a young financial planning prospect, not a seasoned C-level executive with eighteen offices on five continents. He asked me a few questions, then made the tactical call to use the startle method.

What most salespeople fail to realize is that they are not truly selling their product or service. They are selling the product of their product, the service of their service.

What most salespeople fail to realize is that they are not truly selling their product or service. They are selling the product of their product, the service of their service. For instance, when somebody wants to refinance their house, they actually don't want to refinance their house. They want to be able to pay their bills, build a porch on the back of the house, take a vacation, or pay for their kid's tuition.

When you are doing a little do-it-yourself project on the weekend, and you find you need to make a quarter-inch hole in the wall, you go to the hardware store. Why? Are you buying a quarter-inch drill bit, or are you really buying a quarter-inch hole? What the hell do you need a quarter-inch drill bit for unless you need the quarter-inch hole? Now, we're actually connecting. We're also starting to glide into another inherent objection. We're starting to brush the surface, because now we need to talk in terms of the prospect's interests.

In fact, Ben Franklin used this exact rule. He talks about it in his autobiography, which is required reading for all ambitious salespeople. In April of 1755, Franklin was commissioned by General Braddock to secure 150 wagons with four horses on each wagon. The General wanted it for what proved to be an ill-fated expedition against Fort Duquesne. Franklin went to Lancaster and on April 26, 1755, published an advertisement. The purpose of the advertisement was to get farmers interested in supplying wagons. What did it contain? One single paragraph about what Braddock wanted, and six numbered paragraphs about what the farmers would get. Being the good salesperson that he was, Franklin told the farmers how they would benefit from the transaction. Franklin comments in his autobiography on the great and sudden effect it produced and says further, "In three weeks, 150 wagons with 259 carrying horses were on their march for the camp." Suppose instead of arousing the interest of the farmers, he explained what Braddock wanted, as opposed to what the farmers were getting—that's what salespeople do all the time. Braddock had tried to do this before in Maryland on a "we want wagons or else" basis. The net result, Franklin wrote, was twenty-five wagons, some not in serviceable condition.

Last year, over a million quarter-inch drill bits were sold, not because people wanted quarter-inch drill bits but because they wanted quarter-inch holes. Get their interest. Talk holes.

Connecting is what we're trying to do at some level, whether it is through social media, direct interaction face-to-face, on the phone, or any other means. We're trying to overcome the inherent objection of preoccupation.

Last year, over a million quarter-inch drill bits were sold, not because people wanted quarter-inch drill bits but because they wanted quarter-inch holes. Get their interest. Talk holes.

IMPACT STATEMENT

After we resolve the preoccupation, we now need to deal with interest. For this we need an effective Impact Statement to be able to tell our story. The Impact Statement is essentially an elevator pitch. You're trying to get across very succinctly the primary benefits of doing business with you. Salespeople often fail on this point. Without a solid Impact Statement, they walk in with a laundry list of what their company does without making any connection to the buyer. They spray and pray.

This should be a thirty-to-forty-five-second commercial. And like a commercial, the Impact Statement should speak the buyer's language. It needs to tap into the buyer's mind-set, address their needs, and create opportunities.

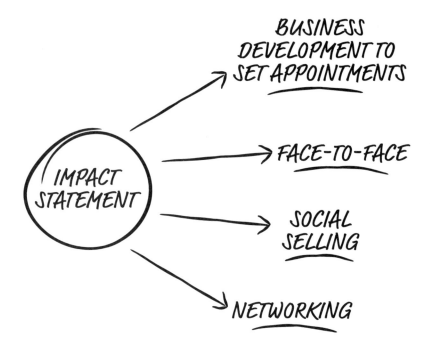

For instance, a financial advisor, like Doug, might say something like: "You know, if you're like a lot of the folks we work with, you're probably looking to sustain your lifestyle over a period of time, get your best return, create an income even as you sleep, ensure the success or legacy of your family. We help our clientele do that by getting a clear understanding of where they are and where they're going. We design and build options for them to execute that long-term plan and, ultimately, we measure results. I don't know if we could do the same for you. Would you mind if I ask you some questions about your financial situation?"

In that example, Doug was able to communicate in a very predictable way. He didn't talk about his financial services business. But he did talk about what his financial services business does for people like the potential client.

The Impact Statement can be used in all sorts of scenarios where a salesperson is trying to cause a result geared toward getting the prospect to open up. That will do two things. It will qualify the prospect to see if they're a good fit for our service, and it will qualify the salesperson in the prospect's eyes, as they judge how the salesperson builds rapport, trust, and understanding of the prospect.

One of the drills that we work on with all salespeople we train is: "Can you tell a prospect or a prospective buyer what you do in less than thirty seconds?"

Let's make a visit back to Walnut Grove for a moment. Remember how I got Mr. Oleson's attention?

"Hey, how do you manage your money every day?"

After he pulls a shotgun on me, I might say quickly, "Mr. Oleson, if you're like most of the mercantile owners that we deal with, you're probably spending time managing your money, balancing your books, and keeping track of who owes you what and what you have to pay out the door. Well, we have a system that calculates a lot of basic things in the moment, saving our customers hours a day that could be better spent at a fishing hole. Now, I'm not sure we can actually solve anything for you, but would you be willing to take a look at it?"

Now, did I talk about a cash register, or did I talk about what a cash register did?

If I were selling accounting software, like QuickBooks, I might get an entrepreneur on the phone and say, "Look, if you're like a lot of entrepreneurs, you're probably concerned with money in, money out, accounts out the door, and taking care of all the taxes and things you're responsible for as a business. We're able to help businesses like yours because we get an understanding of what they're trying to do, what kind of business they're in. We have a couple different versions of software that are less complicated for different kinds of businesses, and then we teach you how to use it so it becomes part of your system. I'm not sure we can do the same thing for you. Do you mind if I ask you a couple of questions, or would you be willing to meet over a cup of coffee?"

You've got to be able to speak on impact and credibility. What can you say about your business that answers what you do, how you do it, and why it would be important to them?

Here's a four-step Impact Statement process:

(**1**) Provide the general benefits you bring to the table.

(**2**) Give a brief overview of how you work or provide an example.

(**3**) Suggest that similar benefits are possible.

(**4**) Get an appointment or advance the sale.

Always remember, the discipline with an Impact Statement is that it can be used to set an appointment.

WHY SPEAK STATEMENT

The last tactic within the connect stage is the Why Speak Statement. The Why Speak Statement is where the salesperson can sit down with a buyer, and create an atmosphere in which the buyer will want to interact with the salesperson.

One of the things the Dallas Cowboys and Cleveland Browns have both installed is an ability to be extremely strong openers. When they're on a conference call, a GoToMeeting or a face-to-face meeting, they try to create an atmosphere in which the potential client will open up about their business. The Cowboys' and Browns' sales people do this by sharing a little bit about their own business.

If you think about it, it makes all kinds of sense. Ever sat down on an airplane and had someone spill their life story to you, inspiring you to do the same right back? To return to the doctor's office, this is what we mean by bedside manner. The more comfortable we are with the practice, the more open we'll be about our lifestyle and how we feel.

In the Why Speak Statement, the salesperson has the uncanny ability to speak about the benefit of the conversation. They'll say things like, "Our conversation today is to talk about how you can leverage some assets of the Dallas Cowboys to ultimately maybe help you drive your business," and then get the buyer to say, "Yeah, that makes sense."

Then the salesperson can continue. "In order to do that, I suggest we talk a little about your role and your business."

That's a next step taken. The salesperson looks the prospect dead in the eye. "Does that make sense?"

The person says yes. All of a sudden, the salesperson has created this environment where both parties are going to connect and qualify each other.

Here's a prime example. One of our good customers is the Dallas Cowboys Partnerships Team, which sells different partnerships such as naming rights to the stadium. We were doing a training/coaching session with their VPs, Brad Burlingame and Scott Erdmann, because one of the big-three accounting firms was interested in leveraging their firm with the Cowboys' brand. They had a phone meeting set, so I asked Scott what his approach would be.

He said he'd start with pleasantries, get into some of the options that he had been thinking about, and then drive to a next step. I coached him to think more strategically, put the ball in their court and use a strong Sales Starter and Impact Statement.

Scott is a pro and very coachable, so when it was game time and the call happened, he got through the pleasantries and immediately asked the partner of the accounting firm how much time he had. From there, Scott told him that the meeting was to discuss how the accounting firm could leverage the Cowboys' brand to increase business. Then Scott launched into his Why Speak Statement, which outlined the context of the call. He provided his bullets:

- First we'll talk about what thoughts you have to see how this can best work.

- Then we'll go over some ideas we have.

- Next we'll agree on the best possible solution.

- And then we'll identify our next steps.

He then asked a Trial Close: "How's that sound?"

The partner of the firm said, "That sounds dead on."

Scott proceeded back to his first question: "How do you see a partnership with the Cowboys working?" The partner went on to outline what it looked like, potential budgets, what they had done in the past. Because Scott used a Why Speak Statement and facilitated the call in the right order, he was able to the get the prospect to outline what business would look like with them and outline their ideas. They say when you negotiate, you're always positioning early to get the other person to go first. In that case, Scott won the meeting.

> They say when you negotiate, you're always positioning early to get the other person to go first.

So at some point, we have to connect and qualify to a point where we can start building rapport. Everyone thinks that sales is about building relationships. Sales is not about relationships. Sales is about rapport. Relationships are an outcome.

Remember, rapport is crucial to sales. Rapport, credibility, and understanding the buyer are three sides of the sales outcome triangle. Everything you say and do, even your appearance, adds credibility or detracts from it. Credibility yields trust, and if you have trust, rapport improves. At the same time, you need to demonstrate that you understand the buyer. When those things happen, in equilateral balance, you sell.

Connecting, however, is the first step toward doing that. It's the step where you overcome preoccupation in the mind of the buyer. You're going to do a much better job at connecting if you remember that it's a two-way street, and put in the practice, time, and effort to perfect your Sales Starters, Impact Statements, and Why Speak Statements.

Then, and only then, can you create the environment that will advance you to that next step: evaluate.

- Prospect's perspective: if you want to sell John Brown what John Brown buys, you've got to see the world through John Brown's eyes.

- It's not about being a great closer, it's about being a great opener.

- You have seven seconds to open somebody's eyes and get their attention, as fast as changing a channel on TV.

- People don't buy your product or service. They buy what it does.

- Don't spray and pray or show up and throw up.

CHAPTER FIVE
Evaluate: Asking the Right Questions

LANCE-ISM #212
"THERE ARE STUPID QUESTIONS."

You don't find your way to the Apple Store by mistake. You went there for a reason. If you make your way onto a car lot, you didn't just wander there by accident.

But the first thing most salespeople ask is: "Can I help you?"

That question is brutal, because the buyer answers the same way each time: "Nope, just looking." It may actually be the dumbest question ever in an unsolicited buy.

The correct question might be: "Have you ever been here before?"

At least that would require you to answer yes or no.

If the shopper says "yes," the salesperson can reply, "Okay then! You would probably like to know about this sale, those things that are on clearance, these new things over here."

But if the shopper says, "No, I've never been here before," the salesperson could say, "Okay then! You would probably like to know about this sale, those things that are on clearance, these new things over here."

You see, it doesn't matter which answer the shopper gives. If the salesperson has a predictable process with directional questions, he or she is automatically tactically superior.

That's why asking a question like: "Can I help you?" is silly. That question right there actually demonstrates that the salesperson thinks it's for them.

My question, however, "Have you ever been here before?" opens up the opportunity to say something like, "If you're like most people who walk in here, this is probably what you want to know."

That's gaining the high ground. And that's the difference between a good salesperson and a great salesperson. A good salesperson thinks they're asking questions for themselves. They're selfish. This is important because when the salesperson asks questions from their own perspective, they end up sounding like a bad episode of *Law and Order*. A great salesperson knows they're asking questions for the buyer.

Thus begins the task of evaluating.

Let's head back to the doctor's office. A patient may think they're healthy. But they may not be right about that. Something may be off. A nurse practitioner or doctor may ask

> A good salesperson thinks they're asking questions for themselves. They're selfish. This is important because when the salesperson asks questions from their own perspective, they end up sounding like a bad episode of Law and Order. A great salesperson knows they're asking questions for the buyer.

questions that lead them to think, "Maybe I'm not as healthy as I need to be."

On the flipside, maybe someone has some false signs leading them to think they're ailing. The doctor's questions can steer them in the direction of thinking, "Hey, I'm actually healthy."

That good doctor, or that medical team, is creating a gap between where a patient is now and where the desired situation. If the gap is very wide, they're creating a solution to get from one point to the other. Essentially, that's what a good salesperson does.

Tactical sales managers will say, "ask open-ended questions," at this point. In truth, it could be open-ended questions, it could be closed-ended questions, it could be essay questions, multiple choice, fill in the blank, or true/false. The key is to create the environment to ask the right questions.

The salesperson asks questions to understand an organization's or individual buyer's current reality. What are the consequences and implications of doing something or not doing something? Ultimately, what's the impact or the payout if something is solved, or an opportunity is fulfilled?

The scenario plays out in most sales situations. It could be as simple as going in to buy a new router. You have an old router that might not be able to handle so much traffic. It's working in certain situations now, but you just added two or three more employees. You have additional traffic. The old router is working, but it's slowing things down. The person looking at routers might not realize that it's possible that they may not need a new router at all. Maybe some kind of new technology would increase efficiency and effectiveness. A good salesperson could figure that out or could help somebody realize that there's some potential for a better solution.

You can bring a horse to water, but you can't make them drink.

But you could put salt in the oats. That's what good questioning does.

If the sales person asks questions the right way, the buyer may give suggestions to how to present a solution, idea, or an opportunity to them. They might actually give the salesperson their version of the solution, idea, or opportunity.

You can bring a horse to water, but you can't make them drink. But you could put salt in the oats. That's what good questioning does.

Picture a river. One bank represents the buyer's current situation, the river represents obstacles, and the other bank is the buyer's desired situation. The purpose of a salesperson's questions is to start building a bridge from the current situation to the desired situation.

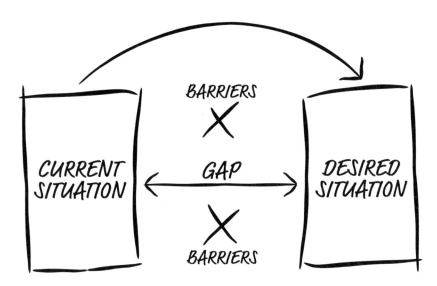

What we as salespeople are trying to do is get the buyer to realize these areas. Once we do, they're open to being persuaded or influenced about anything, whether it be financial planning, that router, or their health.

WHAT'S THE BUYER'S CURRENT REALITY? ASKING THE RIGHT QUESTIONS

The questions a salesperson asks needs to reveal the buyer's current reality. They're the "what" questions. They're questions like: "Tell me about your company. Tell me about your role. Tell me about what brought you into the store here today." They could be anything about the buyer's current reality, or what has happened previously.

In our example about the person shopping for a router, some questions might be: "So, tell me about your current technology. What do you like about it? What don't you like about it? If you had to change something about your current technology, what would you change?"

Say the buyer says they want higher download speeds. Then the salesperson could ask questions geared toward defining an opportunity, like: "What if I told you there's technology that will allow you to bring more people online?"

When we survey salespeople, we ask this question: "Who is the questioning process for, the seller or the buyer?" Most of the time, salespeople would say they're for me as the seller. In reality, they're not. They're actually for the buyer.

Let's explore an experience we've all had—walking onto a car lot. So there you are, browsing in the open lot, and a salesperson approaches.

"Can I help you?" he might ask.

"I'm just looking," you would probably say.

Now, you both know you didn't find your way there by mistake. You didn't just sleepwalk out of bed and end up in a used car lot. It's a stupid question.

What he should say is: "I'm Lance. You are?" And you would give your name.

Then he might go on to say: "Really nice to meet you. If you're like most of the people who walk onto the car lot, you probably know a ton about why you're here and what you're looking for. I don't want to interrupt that thought process, but I just want to give you some idea how we're set up. Over here is pre-owned and over there is new. I'm just here to answer any questions or comments you might have as you look. Hopefully I don't waste your time, you get to see what you're looking for, and you get to ask the questions you need to. Are you more looking for pre-owned or new?"

He would have a better shot there. But if he opens up with a selfish question like, "Can I help you?" he's going to lose ground. And when you lose ground in sales, you lose sales.

Now, take that and complicate it by about tenfold in a B2B sale. The salesperson must be able to open really well. That goes back to our qualifying stage, but then they have to ask the right questions. Remember, it's not about just asking questions. It's about asking the right questions.

The way the salesperson knows how to ask the right question is to start with the current situation and the desired situation. The salesperson is looking for the current situation, obstacles, and impact of the desired situation. A skilled salesperson is trying to see through the buyer's eyes. If I can see things through the buyer's eyes, I can sell to what the buyer buys. As the salesperson brings the buyer through this questioning process, they will be asking questions in the right combination. The salesperson is going to ask more current situation questions, because they're the easiest questions for the buyer.

If I were selling financial services, I might say, "Tell me a little bit about what your philosophy is on how you put money away for your future. What does your nest egg look like? Is it good, bad, or ugly? What's your philosophy? What's your current 401(k) look like? Let's look a little bit in the future. You're thinking about retirement. What should it be? What are you looking to do? When are you looking to retire?"

I'm going to ask these questions where I cause these gaps between the current and desired situations. I'm going to ask way more current situation questions, and then start asking for the desired situation. After that, I'll ask the buyer about some things that are in the way. They might say, "I've got to meet my bills now, I can't put 10 percent away."

And that gives me the opportunity for more questions. "Well, if you don't do that now, what's going to ultimately happen if you don't start doing it now?"

They might say, "I'm going to be in a scenario where I'm not where I need to be. I'm going to be racing towards the end and I might run out of time if I don't start doing it now."

In this situation, I'm going to ask questions around the three E's: elementary, evaluative, and elaborative questions.

Elementary questions could be: "What color? Which one?" Elaborative questions include: "How so?" An evaluative question is: "What's your opinion on *x*?"

I'm going to ask essay questions, true/false questions, fill in the blank questions, yes or no questions. And at the end, I might say, "If I'm hearing it right, you'd be comfortable if you had a plan to ramp up how to get toward retirement. So, you'd be open to that?"

This questioning process is our ability to interact. In some complex sales processes, this could be a whole meeting. This could be several meetings or more as the prospect adds decision makers, because complex B2B processes right now have anywhere from three to four influencers, sideliners, a champion, and then, ultimately, a buyer. We might be collecting this evaluation over a few engagements, or it might be during the very first connection.

I recently started working out again, so I decided to seek out a gym. There is a big Lifetime Fitness near my house that has a pool, a spa, and you can even get your nails done. You can get food there, go rock-climbing, and do yoga. Free weights. Basketball. Cardio equipment. You name it; they have it.

As I went to weigh out the gym vs. the local rec center, the options were overwhelming. So I sat down with the GM of Lifetime Fitness, and he said, "Can I ask you a few questions before I give you the tour? What are you doing or not doing as it relates to fitness? I'll show you what we have and see if we may be a fit. Then we'll go from there."

He used a great Why Speak Statement. His questions revolved around four things:

1. How often I work out.

2. If I had any workout equipment at home.

3. What I thought I should or could be doing more of. What's the ideal situation? Meaning, how much I should be working out.

4. What I was looking for.

"So what's been holding you back? Why hasn't that been happening?" he asked.

I said, "Quite frankly, time."

He nodded. "What else?"

"Probably know-how," I said. "That's why I'm here."

"If you did have that access, what would be the perceived benefit?" he asked.

"I'd be healthier."

Essentially what he did was sell to a gap. He sold to my desired situation, rather than to my current situation. Lifetime Fitness was a vehicle to get from where I was to where I wanted to be. It wasn't necessarily going to solve the problem, but it was the vehicle to get me there. Incidentally, both my son and I now have memberships.

It's really not that much different than what a doctor does at a visit. When we are sick and go in, the doctor or nurse gets our weight, blood pressure, looks at our history up to that point. They look to see what it should be, barriers or the causes for the discrepancy. Then they look for a potential payout, and provide a prescription to fill that gap.

We do business with a lot of employee benefit organizations that sell pretty complex insurance packages to companies to support their employee's healthcare benefits. One of the companies we've worked with over the years, McGohan Brabender, actually follows the same model as Lifetime Fitness. Every year they look to renew our business so they look at how many employees we have, our current claims, what has changed in our business, how much our business is the same this year vs. the previous year. They look at the direction the company is headed in and forecast changes.

For the current situation, they look at our existing insurance— what we used, what we didn't use. They look at what's changing in our business. What we need more of or less of. They are constantly getting us to look at the gaps between how we're doing business now, how things will change, and how insurance affects that. What are the obstacles and barriers? Then, if we address that gap, what's the payout? Scott McGohan, the CEO, is very successful in his own right. He has a well-honed machine with his sales team and their process of asking the right questions in the right order to make the best recommendations for their clients. If you think about it, this questioning model is a way to solve problems and address primary interest and buying motive, because it sells to a gap. Other people call it addressing pain or discomfort. Sometimes it's a need. Sometimes it's an opportunity. But it's always about asking the right questions.

Let's run through an exercise on asking the right questions: Pick a number between two and nine. If you can't add, subtract, or multiply, pick a low number. Got your number? Now take your number and multiply it by nine. You should have two integers.

Next, take those two numbers and add them together. Whatever that answer is, now subtract five.

Are you with me so far? So with A as 1, B as 2, C as 3, D as 4, and E as 5, select the letter in the alphabet that corresponds with your number. Everybody got it? With your letter in the alphabet, pick a state in the union, or a country in Europe that begins with that letter.

Okay, now using the second letter of your state or country, pick an animal that begins with that letter. For those people counting with their toes, make sure to put your shoes back on.

So did you pick Delaware? Denmark? Elephant? How about Elk? Or Emu? Eels?

Pretty freaking cool, right?

So who was making all the decisions in that example? You or me? I was just asking questions. *You* were the one making all the decisions. I just limited your scope with each question. I set foul lines. I didn't ask a question that was one to a thousand. I said to pick a number between two and nine because every time we do the math, it comes out to be the same thing.

The problem with selling is that most salespeople don't have a predictable process to build a predictable result in asking questions. Therefore, every time they go to ask questions, they start over again and again.

But if you're being really smart, you go back to your Why Speak Statement. If your agenda is solid and your Why Speak Statement is sound, you're literally creating those boundaries from the get go.

Remember, a good lawyer and a good salesperson never ask questions they don't know the answer to.

> **Remember, a good lawyer and a good salesperson never ask questions they don't know the answer to.**

So as we ask questions, we've got to have a process. We've got to think about what types of questions we ask and how we ask those questions and lead the buyer towards an answer, much like the Socratic method.

When trying to get someone to see his point of view, Socrates would engage people in deep dialogues, asking a series of seemingly innocuous questions that slowly created a sense of common ground between him and the other person. Once enough common ground was established, the dissenter had no choice but to agree with Socrates' perspective.

That's what made Socrates the ultimate salesman. He understood the process of evaluation. And ultimately, evaluation all comes down to the Sales Song. You know the Sales Song, right? Wait a minute, you never heard the Sales Song? How can you possibly sell if you don't know the Sales Song? Everybody knows the Sales Song!

Alright, if you've never heard it, here is how it goes. The tune sounds kind of like "The Wheels on the Bus." Feel free to sing out loud, even if you're reading this on an airplane. There are bound to be others around you who will join in. Ready?

What do they want, and why do they want it?
What do they want, and why do they want it?
What do they want and why do they want it,
all the way to the close!

Salespeople need to ask questions around those two main factors. And we, as salespeople, need to get better at asking the questions that will help us understand a prospect's needs. Equally as important, however, we need to help prospects see the wisdom of considering our solution, also known as the diagnosis.

- Get biblical. Ask and you shall receive.

- Shut up and listen.

- Question to the gap.

- Let the other person think it's their idea. It's harder for a buyer to argue their own idea.

CHAPTER SIX

Diagnose: Making Your Idea Their Idea

Not long ago I saw a U2 concert at Hard Rock Stadium with my family. We were down in the club level and all these Miami Dolphins salespeople were talking to me, and I spotted this one particular guy who works there as the head of the sponsorship. Actually, he's kind of hard to miss. He's like 6'4", looks like an Abercrombie model, a really good-looking kid. So I was talking to him and I looked down at his shoes, and I said to myself *Dude, he has a nice pair of Adidas AlphaBounces on.* They were white, soft, the kind of shoe that looks cool as hell but comfortable, too.

So the next day at the pool I turned to my wife, Lisa. "Remember when we were talking to the salespeople at the Miami Dolphins?"

"Yeah," she said. "You mean before the concert, when we were eating food and having a couple?"

"Right," I said. "Remember the one guy, Ryan? The really tall guy?"

"Oh, the really good-looking kid?" she asked.

"Yeah," I said, feigning indifference. "But did you see the sneakers he had on?"

"No, what were they?"

"They were white Adidas AlphaBounces."

She just looked at me for a beat. "There's no way you're going to pull white sneakers off. Have you seen you lately?"

I couldn't believe she went there. "Really?"

"Dude, you're not that good looking."

"Come on!"

She found a stroke of mercy. "Look, you shouldn't wear white shoes. You'll just have them dirty in, like, a day."

So then I was just sitting there asking myself questions, assessing my situation: *Should I get new sneakers? Do I need new sneakers? What kind of new sneakers do I want? What kind do I already have?*

Three or four days later I was back in Columbus, having lunch with one of our staff members, Lauren.

"Hey," I said to her. "I have to run over to the mall after lunch. Do you have some time to just go over there with me so I don't have to drop you off at the office first and then go back?"

Lauren nodded. "No, no it's right here. Go. What are you getting?"

"I'm looking at a pair of kicks, a pair of sneakers."

"Oh, okay. Cool. What are you thinking?"

I shrugged nonchalantly. "I'm thinking of white Adidas AlphaBounce."

Her eyes bug. "White? Really? You?"

It was a conspiracy. "What the hell? You friggin' talk to Lisa?"

Eventually she conceded and so I went to the mall, looking for some kicks. As I was looking at the white AlphaBounces, the salesman approaches.

"What size are you?"

"I'm a 9 1/2 or 10," I replied. "Can you bring them both out?"

He disappeared into the back. In the meantime, Lauren picked up a pair of smoke-gray AlphaBounces.

"You might want to look at these," she said.

"Are you texting Lisa right now," I said with a sneer.

"No," she said. "I've just been around you long enough to know you're actually kind of dirty."

So with my self-esteem waning, I told the salesman, "All right, give me these gray ones, too."

At this point I was putting them on and asking myself questions: Do I want the white ones more now out of sheer revenge because two people said no? Or are they right? But what if they are wrong? Should I follow my instinct?

So the guy brought out a 9 1/2 and a 10. I tried the 10, then I slipped on the 9 1/2.

"Well, what do you think?" he asked.

I shake my head. "I don't know if I want the 9 1/2 or the 10."

"You should get the 10," he said, "because when you work out, your feet will swell a little bit and they'll expand."

"No, no, no," I said from behind a grin. "These aren't for working out."

We were connected at that point. He evaluated my need based on a few questions. Now came the time for the diagnosis.

He smiled. "Oh, they're *those* sneakers. Then you definitely need to get the 9 1/2. You just want to be able to slip those bad boys on, right? Not worrying about them slipping off or tying them up tight. Just wear them nice and loose."

"Right," I said, pausing for a moment. "What color would *you* get?"

"Eh, the white ones are gonna get dirty, a lot dirtier than the other ones, and quicker unless you're super-careful. I'd get the gray ones. They give off the same effect."

In that scenario, I went and bought something in an unsolicited buy. But I still asked myself several sets of questions: *What's the current situation? What's the desired situation? What should I get? What are my options? Should I get them? Should I not get them?*

And the salesperson took my answers, my questions, and my desires into consideration to come up with a diagnosis for me—the need I had to fill, or the problem I had to solve, or the opportunity I wanted to create.

THE BUYER'S MOTIVE

Let's go back to our doctor's office analogy.

The questions the doctor asks are simple at first. They're based off of history and they're based off of what is known. What's your age? When is the last time you've been to the doctor? How do you feel right now? The questions get more complicated as they move on. Then he or she weighs my answers to figure out what problem might need fixing. Then based off the doctor's, or in our case the salesperson's, expertise, they can arrive at a diagnosis. That's the kind of process we're following.

The salesperson should be able to determine through the line of questioning during the evaluation stage what the prospect's buying absolutes are. The seller should also be able to determine the things that are optional. Then, the savvy salesperson should be able to take a product or service and talk to the specific motivations of the individual buyer. or the group of buyers.

Buying criteria could be price, terms of the deal, favorable interest rates, or whether the buyer can go forward with no money down. Certain financing options could come into play, ease of use, or an all-inclusive package.

Some of those criteria are need-to-have. Others are nice-to-have. Some are absolutes. It's very possible that absolutes get mixed up sometimes, so be wary. To diagnose properly, we really need to pay attention to what those absolutes are as we ask our questions. Then we need to figure out the buyer's motive—the reason a buyer wants something.

Individual motives will typically conform in one way or another to Maslow's hierarchy of needs—physical survival, safety, love and belonging, esteem and self-actualization—at some level. It's a concept that has been around since the 1940s, and it's usually shown as a pyramid, with basic physiological needs at the bottom, and above them, some higher-order psychological needs.

Remember, we are all emotional beings, and a salesperson sells to people. And people buy emotionally, but justify their decision using logic. That's why the salesperson has to know those factors. It's not an exact science. But those questions we worked through during the evaluation period helps the salesperson put the jigsaw puzzle together.

But just because people buy on emotion doesn't mean you need to sell that way. In the sales process, always use logic and reasoning, not emotion.

Imagine I'm a doctor who is dealing with a really young patient under seven years old. For whatever reason, she's in a lot of pain. I'm really going to have to see what she sees, to understand her through asking questions, because I can't feel her pain. I can't make an informed diagnosis if I'm focused on feelings instead of facts.

Remember, in sales, relationships are outcomes, and I think it's nearly impossible to be really empathetic. Just like a doctor, a salesperson should not try to be empathetic.

When I went to college, the only way I was going to be able to get a scholarship was to become a resident assistant. I realized if I became an RA, I'd get room and board paid for. What a great gig. I really didn't know what I was getting myself into. Ultimately, they taught this concept called Counseling 302, where we really had to understand that we might have people on our floor that could be dealing with all kinds of issues. To be honest, I didn't take it very seriously. I was more like Mel Gibson from the first *Lethal Weapon* movie.

Remember in the movie when Mel Gibson and Danny Glover had a jumper on top of a building? The dude was going to commit suicide and Mel Gibson went up there and was like, "just jump." The guy was taken aback. Then Mel handcuffed himself to the guy to call his bluff and said, "You wanna jump. We're going to jump."

I would have been Mel before I went to Counseling 302. I didn't quite grasp the concept that people really had mental challenges. I based everything off of my own experiences. I would have told the poor guy to jump. Or said, "Just stop eating, man. You'll die. Mission accomplished."

After going through Counseling 302 though, I realized that people have some deep-seated things they have to deal with. I gained a healthy respect. We had to go through this project where we had to do counseling and ask the right questions. That's when I learned how important empathy is.

It takes such a deep-seated connection to be empathetic. Empathy's hard; you and I would literally need to jump off the side of the building together, hold hands, live, and ask each other how we felt afterward. It's hard to do. In many sales situations that I've seen over the years, empathy is not something you want to do. If a salesperson is truly being empathetic, they won't necessarily challenge the buyer when the process moves to an open-objection or negotiation phase. There's just no room for empathy in sales.

Instead, I live from the Dale Carnegie side of things. I think you should be sympathetic to people's ideas and desires, because, after all, they birthed them. You wouldn't tell someone who just had a newborn baby that their kid was ugly. I mean, I've seen some ugly kids, but I would never tell a new mother that her kid was ugly. Why? Because she birthed that baby.

We spend a lot of time in selling and managing, callously telling people that their ideas are wrong. But we never give the consideration that they birthed them. I think the concept that we can always revisit as salespeople is to try to honestly see things from the other person's point of view. For me, that's the most important rule out of the thirty rules in the book *How to Win Friends and Influence People*.

LEADING THE BUYER TO THE GAP

Now, let's get into things a little bit deeper. When I sell any product or service, I could be solving a need, or I could be creating an opportunity. But diagnosing is a delicate business. Essentially, we need to tell our prospect in a nice way that their kid is ugly. As salespeople, we are identifying that gap between where someone is and where they need to be. This essentially implies a problem exists, a change needs

> **Diagnosing is a delicate business. Essentially, we need to tell our prospect in a nice way that their kid is ugly.**

to happen, or a commitment of some kind is required. And we also have to be careful when stating our diagnosis, because we don't want to make somebody feel the pain or implication of not being able to do something.

Have you ever been at a nice restaurant with people you wanted to impress, and so you order a fine Napa Cab, only to have the sommelier come back with an alternative bottle because the one you ordered was out of stock? There's that moment of sheer panic when they have selected something way out of your price range, though it's too awkward to address at the moment. A good salesperson would have read the situation and brought out a comparable bottle. A bad salesperson might take the opportunity to stick you with a $400 Merlot that has been sitting in the cellar for twenty years by either banking on the fact that you wouldn't ask the price in front of your guests, or by guilting you into it if by chance you did happen to ask.

Manipulating and guilting someone into a buy is just a sucky way to do business. Period.

The key to good diagnosing is leading the buyer to the gap, and, ultimately, if you asked the right questions, you can actually make it their idea. It's a lot harder for someone to walk away from their own idea than it is from your idea.

We recently had the opportunity to pitch to an iconic pro-sports team, the Boston Red Sox (Fenway Sports Management). We had initial meetings with senior-level executives and got to meet with their EVP of Sales and Operations, John Clark. In this meeting, John did a wonderful job describing the historical significance of Fenway Park, how his business ran at all levels, their sales philosophy, how they were managed, how they sold and marketed, and how the marketplace perceived them. As we guided them through the questions about his current and past situations, it became easy for him to talk about things needing change and what needed to get better.

We also asked him, if he were in our position, how would he approach training his sales team and coaching his sales managers. He was then able to talk specifically about the same things, but in the desired situation. He told us where he was, where he wants to go, and how he would approach things if he were us.

We came back to him a few weeks later with a tailored discussion document (proposal). Our first two pages listed the things he said about his current and desired situations. Essentially, we showed him the gap between where he currently was and where he wanted to be. Our most junior salesperson prepared this document and verbalized the findings and the gap. Our recommendations were based on his ideas—remember, it's hard to argue your own ideas. It would be like going into a doctor's office, getting an exam and finding out how sick you are, your weight, blood pressure, all your vitals, as opposed to what they should be. The remedy, or prescription, is more of a realization and becomes the buyer's idea.

The skillful salesperson designs questions to help buyers come to the realization that there might be an opportunity to fill a gap, or maybe a need to solve or resolve. There might be a better solution than what they already have, or better product/service than they already have. As the salesperson and buyer do that, they come to a diagnosis together.

For example, say a financial services buyer is trying to save money and plan for their future. Why are they doing that? Well, they want to survive in the future. Maybe they have a fear of not having things, of dying with no money in their hand. What are their criteria? Maybe they can only afford to devote 5 percent of their income to their 401(k) or anything else. A consideration that might be nice to have in this scenario is a low-fee or no-fee situation. The salesperson is trying to find out about those things as they ask questions.

The diagnosis then is the ability to actually present to certain buying motivations and to tailor an offering.

THE SPECIFIC INTEREST STATEMENT

To make the right diagnosis, the salesperson has to be able to make interim summaries throughout the process, to say something like: "Based on what you're saying, you're looking to address your number one or number two interest, and that's going to address your motivation."

This is where the salesperson makes a Specific Interest Statement. He or she can apply the product or service to the buyer's needs to appeal to both the buyer's logical and emotional reasons for buying.

As the salesperson asks questions, they're going to categorize information for a diagnosis. To do that, we as salespeople are going to find out the buyer's number one, number two, and number three interests and opportunities. At the same time, our questions help the buyer see our eventual diagnosis and prescription as more of a priority.

In our financial services example, for instance, the buyer may go from thinking, "Hey, I don't have any time or really the extra money to start investing in my financial future," to, "I can't afford not to do it. I've never weighed it out. The implications are too vast to start later. I need to start now." That change flows from the salesperson's questioning.

The number one opportunity is what the buyer wants. Then the salesperson has to find out why they want it. That's their motive. In some training, it's called the emotional hot button. Essentially, the salesperson is selling to what the buyer wants and why they want it. Then the buyer is going to have absolutes, such as price, and those absolutes shape the buyer's priorities. For instance, if price is an absolute, a buyer may want something with all the bells and whistles but sacrifice bells and whistles for something they see as necessary. The buyer might not only have one motive, but several motives. Just as well, they might not have one absolute, but a few absolutes.

If you confuse an absolute with an influencer, or you confuse a number two with a three priority without hitting the buyer's number one, you risk hurting their urgency. That's why it's crucial to lay the proper groundwork before offering a diagnosis, which requires rapport and asking the right questions.

As I've mentioned earlier, one of our good customers, McGohan Brabender, is one of the largest privately held insurance companies in the country. Over the years we've done a lot of sales training and sales management consulting with them. When Obamacare (ACA) was introduced, the law was almost 11,000 pages, standing at three feet tall. This changed the game of selling insurance to businesses. Buyers suddenly re-aligned their criteria and influencers to do business with a broker. The senior management at McGohan Brabender, Scott McGohan and Mike Suttman, wanted to change the way their sales-people approached these buying influencers and criteria.

First, the buyers wanted consulting to decipher the cryptic and often confusing law. Second, they wanted to know that the broker had leverage for negotiating with the insurance company. Third, they wanted to know how the broker could leverage wellness to insure a healthier lifestyle for employees, while reducing claims. Fourth, when there was just-in-time advice needed, would that broker be there?

Adding to the level of complexity is the fact that there are multiple decision makers involved in these types of decisions; far more than in the past because of stronger financial concerns. So at any one time, one of McGohan Brabender's salespeople could be dealing with a CEO, CFO, VP of HR, or HR manager. Each one of these decision makers could have any of these four as their absolute or criteria. So the risk is this: if you find yourself talking to all of these people, but just to the influencers and not to their criteria, you could lose the deal.

Think about the car lot. While you are browsing the new and used models, you have your buying criteria, and the reason you're buying a car. Maybe that reason is to get to work, or to get your family back and forth. If you need a car in order to get to work, you're buying that car for survival in some sense. If you're buying because you want to taxi your family around town, you might be thinking about safety features over what is cheap and convenient.

You have absolutes in this car buying process. There are certain things you can and can't afford. Pricing, monthly payments, interest rates, or a combination of those things can make the difference in the buying process.

This knowledge allows the salesperson to talk specifically to the buyer's needs. If the buyer's priority is safety, for instance, they might be willing to forego a Bluetooth connection between their phone and the car in favor of a safety feature.

But remember, most unsolicited buyers don't go into a sales situation realizing that they have these issues or opportunities the salesperson is diagnosing. So that means the diagnosis is about our ability as a salesperson to look somebody in the eye no matter what kind of sale it is and say, "Listen, based on what you're saying, you're trying to address this, and this will allow you to get your payout." And that is what actually helps us tailor what we do, and that's truly what a diagnosis is. It's our best-educated suggestion.

It's up to the salesperson to get the buyer to acknowledge that the factors they outlined are correct, and then get the buyer to a point where they would be willing to listen to specific suggestions for addressing those factors. The diagnosis is about getting somebody to say, "Yes, I'll allow you to present further, because what you say makes sense to me."

Once the buyer says that, the salesperson can move on to the prescription. But keep in mind, the right solution for the wrong problem is worse than the wrong solution to the right problem.

- People buy the product of our product and service of our service, not what it is or what it means.

- People buy from people. To sell is human.

- It's not about empathy, it's about being sympathetic to someone's ideas.

- Prospects like to buy a tailored solution, not a one-size-fits-most solution.

CHAPTER SEVEN
Prescribe: The Right Solution for the Right Problem

LANCE-ISM #309
"YOU HAVE TWO EARS AND ONE MOUTH FOR A REASON."

O nce the salesperson has diagnosed the problem correctly, he or she needs to present the right prescription in such a way that it persuades the buyer to see value in the solution or opportunity. As salespeople, we need to gain the high ground in order to overcome doubt quickly and effectively. And what inherently overcomes doubt? Evidence.

Early in my career, a moving company that specialized in moving older furniture wanted to work with my mentor and me to boost the effectiveness of their salespeople.

"What's the biggest objection you get?" I asked the sales manager.

The sales manager, the VP of sales, and the president all responded. "Price. We just get killed on price."

"So what's the difference between you and other moving companies?" I asked, and they scratched their head. I said, "You want us to come in and do training on price? That's easy. Just deal with price. Look, you have to do something."

Then my mentor, Sam Iorio, said, "You guys have been in business this long and you're just getting killed by the competition. There's more competition than ever before."

"Yeah, a lot of people are starting to get in our space," said the sales manager.

Sam replied, "So what I understand is you specialize more in antiques, older types of things. You don't do office moving."

The president chimed in. "Right. We work with estates and that type of thing. Family members of people who have passed away."

I jumped in. "So the stuff's valuable."

We pressed again. "There has to be something you do different," said Sam.

I looked at them. "There has to be something about your business that's different from everyone else. Is it how you do it?"

The VP of sales shook his head. "No. I mean, moving's moving."

"Is it how you interact with the people?" I asked.

"No," said the sale manager. "A lot of this stuff is through a request. We kind of find the address. We do a little bit of a diagnostic, a little bit of an evaluation."

"Well, what's your pricing?" I asked.

"Well, we're about 15-20 percent higher than everybody else," said the VP of sales.

"Okay," I said, giving it some thought. "Well, how much damage is done, typically, when anybody moves? If I just hired Atlas Movers, is there damage?"

"Yeah, there's always damage," said the sales manager. "At least 5-10 percent of the contents get damaged."

"Well, that's interesting," I said. "So why are you guys more expensive?"

"We usually have less damage than anybody else," said the sales manager.

I sat forward. "Can you prove it?"

"Yeah," said the sales manager. "We can prove it a little bit."

"Why do you have less damage than anybody else?" I asked.

The owner proudly stepped up. "Lance, it's because of how we equip our trucks."

"What do you mean? How you equip your trucks?" I asked.

"We actually have three trucks," he said. "And we have specially manufactured shocks on our trucks that actually control things around the cobblestones and winding roads around Philly."

"Show me how," I said.

"This is the way I used to sell them," he said. "This is what I do."

Out of his desk he pulled a balloon. He blew it up halfway. "You know what, Lance? This is how we equip our trucks. Our shock system is like this balloon. If you can imagine your contents, the truck is my top hand, the road surface is my bottom hand, and between is that shock. If we hit any bumps or turns, our system absorbs all these blows and actually reduces damage significantly. We'll put our money on it. That's why we charge more."

My jaw dropped. "Do your salespeople sell like that?"

"Well, they talk about it."

"No. Do they show people like you just showed me?"

He laughed. "No. They tell me it's old-school."

"You guys need to start doing that in your presentations every time, without fail," I said. "People need to understand that. You've got to substantiate that."

That's using evidence and being persuasive. That's the salesperson delivering a prescription in a way meant to convince. That's gaining the high ground.

> **Using evidence and being persuasive. That's the salesperson delivering a prescription in a way meant to convince.**

OVERCOMING DOUBT

As salespeople, we have to use some form of evidence to help convince the buyer, to persuade and influence. Remember, everything from here on out relies on the three elements of our Specific Interest Statement. Now that we have that foundation, we need to climb our way to the top of the mountain through evidence, facts, practical applications, and benefits of our prescription.

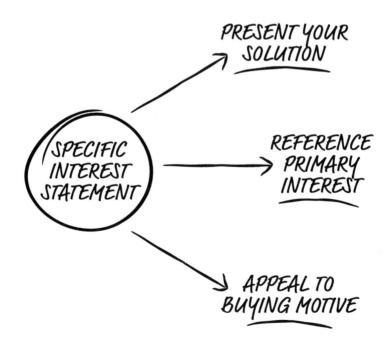

And the inherent objection right now is doubt. I don't mean the doubt in the salesperson's abilities or solution necessarily, though that certainly is a real factor. Right now, I'm talking about the buyer, the prospect, the patient, doubting whether or not they even have an issue, whether or not they necessarily agree with what's going on. Many times, they're going to wrestle with the question: "Do I even need to do anything?"

Be mindful, change is hard. At the end of the day, we as salespeople often sell change.

When I'm teaching in a classroom, I notice that lots of people fold their hands. I'll ask them all to fold their hands naturally, like in a praying position. Then I'll ask them how it feels, and undoubtedly they all agree that it feels good, comfortable. Then I'll tell them to move their fingers up a rung or down a rung, and then ask how it feels. They always remark that it feels strange. It feels different. That feels like somebody else's hand. A lot of times we're selling people a way to do something differently. We're trying to get them to change. And if we go back to buying motives, we revisit Maslow's hierarchy of needs. Most motives go under those needs. They exist corporately and individually. So if we're selling change, it is imperative that we address the motivational factors.

So the prescription has to deal with the specific situation. Just like a doctor isn't going to prescribe you every medicine ever invented, you can't necessarily pitch everything in your product arsenal. Yet most salespeople have a tendency to throw a bunch of solutions up on the wall and hope something sticks.

Recently, we were talking to a group from Adobe. They were telling us one of the biggest issues that they have is when they're selling their software to measure the impact of certain advertising return on investment (ROI), their salespeople have a tendency to spit out all the benefits of what the software does.

Actually, when you just spit out a bunch of benefits or opportunities and you just say something like, "Hey, here are some of the outcomes that you can achieve," it actually causes more doubt. Ultimately, what we're trying to do is give somebody specific enough information and just enough to help them make a buying decision. More is not always better.

Over the last few years, we've done business with over sixty-five pro-sports clients and fifteen clients from the insurance industry. We've trained nearly two thousand salespeople and found one thing to be true—they all lean on two types of evidence: stats and examples. They rarely ever dig deep to use any other form of evidence.

Well, there are all kinds of ways to use evidence, like doing a demo, giving an example, using facts, an exhibit, analogies, testimonials, and statistics. A demo is a physical demonstration with the proper model to illustrate your prescription, like the moving company. In an example, you're providing the buyer with a relevant story about a satisfied customer. A fact is something current about the market. An exhibit can be graphs, charts, materials, photos, or other materials that show evidence to support the salesperson's solution. Analogy is when you're comparing your solution to another situation that the buyer might be familiar with. A testimonial is third-party confirmation (video, written, it could be anything). Statistics is the use of accurate, relevant numbers to support your solution.

Remember Doug with the nest egg analogy? That was not just an analogy; it was a physical prop. This guy was one of the best Merrill Lynch people in the country, and that's why he's successful. He was able to teach, tailor, and convince me with a certain form of evidence.

As salespeople, we use the SEES model: stats, examples, exhibits, and stories.

(S)TATS

(E)XAMPLES

(E)XHIBITS

(S)TORIES

If we go back to our medical conversation, there are probably a lot of things a doctor can do to make somebody better. But at some level, if they do more, they're going to cause confusion and doubt. When possible, a doctor is going to keep their prescription simple, straightforward, and convincing.

A salesperson needs to do the same thing.

Unfortunately, that's not what happens. Salespeople have a bad habit of overwhelming their prospects with details in the hope that one or two may stick.

We were just talking to the group that does licensing for the NBA. If a tie manufacturer, for example, wanted to use NBA logos, they would pitch the NBA on why they should partner with them. A lot of leagues do this, and a lot of organizations do stuff like it. One of the things the people in this group realize is the more they pitch, the more useless information they overload. They find holes in the presentation because they over-pitch things. That's when doubt comes in.

> **Salespeople have a bad habit of overwhelming their prospects with details in the hope that one or two may stick.**

GET YOUR LAWYER ON: USE EVIDENCE

More information is not better. We want to get the need or the issue right and give them enough information to feed that. The problem is most salespeople don't follow a process. They don't do a good job of making sure on the diagnosis. They don't say, "If I understand things right, you're looking to reduce the amount of time it takes you to determine the ROI on this advertising, at the same time making decisions about what the best one to use is. Is that right?"

Most salespeople speak in gaping generalities, and that's actually what causes doubt. What does a lawyer use to convince a jury or a judge? They use evidence, and salespeople have a tendency not to use the right evidence.

If I were going to prescribe a drug, I'm going to tell you about the pill, its size, color when to take it, how to take it, and give you the instructions with it. You, as a patient, should start to feel a little bit better. Because what happens is if we can communicate the right way and we can communicate about our product or service the right way, we actually answer the questions in the buyer's mind to help convince them that we're the right solution or the right opportunity.

If you get into every buyer's mind, you'll find five specific questions you need to resolve:

(1) What is it?

(2) How does it work?

(3) Why is it important?

(4) Who says so, besides you?

(5) Can you prove it?

So when you promote a prescription, the buyer is not just going to accept a wink and a promise. They're going to look for different forms of evidence. They're going to look for third party validation.

Say you were the general manager of a hotel, and the hotel was looking to do a lot of restoration, big capital expenditure kind of stuff. You know that you renovate all of the rooms, their fixtures and appliances. Well, sooner or later, you're going to have to get to the carpet. But the carpet is a big capital investment. You aren't going to start with the carpet, because you're going to have to do so much contracting that it would likely get destroyed in the process. And the carpet isn't necessarily bad. It needed to be improved, but it isn't nasty, puce shag with vomit stains or anything.

Let's say the biggest carpeted areas in your hotel are your banquet areas. And say, for instance, I was in there selling you chairs. The chairs have to be updated, because they are the oldest things, not to mention the things that people touch all the time. If I am selling you chairs and I find out that you want to replace the carpet over time while you were doing other capital investments, I could somehow tie my sale of catering chairs to you, and to the overall project.

I might go in, and say, "I learned in my evaluation diagnosis that you're doing capital investments. You prioritized to me what you were going to do in the hotel. Update the furniture first, some construction, but you're hoping to get at least two to three more years out of the carpets, because that was the last thing you were going to invest in. Plus, there's going to be a lot of traffic on them as you do construction."

You would naturally agree, because I'm just talking facts at that point. Now I could go on to say, "Let me show you a few of these chairs. What's interesting about this particular chair in front of you right now is that it has a forty-five minute cushion on it. That means after about forty-five minutes, your guests will probably have to get up and resituate themselves. The really interesting thing, though, is that these chairs have four stainless steel discs at the bottom that actually rotate 360 degrees. They are also multi-directional, based on how you're leaning on them. The four stainless steel discs allow for them to slide, to glaze the carpet, almost like ice. It has less friction, which will cause your carpet to wear and tear less. Let me show you how that works."

I've answered what the chair is, how it works, and now, since I tied it to saving the carpet, I've actually made the chair a long-term capital investment, thereby answering why it's important.

We have to be able to communicate in a way that answers those five questions. If we don't, we don't erase doubt, but actually increase it.

And, just as important as what we present, how we present ties into credibility and believability. If you sell face to face, people are going to judge you on how you look. Like it or not, business is like high school on steroids. They're going to judge you on how you look, how you dress, how you present yourself, how you communicate, how you deal with people. The last thing people will judge you on is who you are as an individual. It's a shame, but that's just the way it is.

The next thing on trial is your enthusiasm. Some salespeople just aren't very good at being enthusiastic. They're like crypt keepers, or like stone. The root word of enthusiasm is *enthous*, which in Greek means "God from within." So many salespeople don't sell very well because they're not enthusiastic. It's not about being a cheerleader. The last for letters in enthusiasm, is I-A-S-M. When we deliver the solution, that means: "I Am Sold, Myself."

A lot of salespeople fail at this when they present the prescription. They're not actually sold themselves on what they do. And on top of that, they don't know enough about the customer, so they don't speak in specifics or they mindlessly rattle off statistics and general facts. They're not good storytellers, or good at using props. They lean too much on a PowerPoint, and they let that be the presentation. That's not our presentation. *We're* the presentation, the messenger.

An effective salesperson has to use forms of evidence to convince people. They have to be great storytellers and be great at analogies.

But there are other things that help us become a powerful communicator, too. How we look, what we say, even the order we say things in, will help persuade a prospect or sow doubt in their mind.

Say I was trying to convince a township or city council to control the deer population. I could say, "You know, we should actually really think about killing at least 20 percent of the deer population. I say that because right now, in our city, deer have caused at least five near-death experiences, countless dollars of damage to property, cars and homes alike. We're teetering on the brink of losing human lives because the deer population's out of control. I think we should actually kill deer to save lives."

That's one way to pitch it. That might appeal to the hunter in the room. But I've got to think of my audience.

Another way to do it, same argument, is to open like this:

"Two of my sons and I were a little south of Cleveland toward end of fall. It was right around dusk, just about 6:15 or so in the evening, right when it started to get dark, so cars were just starting to turn their lights on.

"I was heading south, and suddenly this deer jetted off on the passenger side, right in front of my car. I slammed on the brakes. My younger son in the back was leaning forward. He had his seatbelt on, but actually, as I hit my brakes hard, he slammed his face into the front of the seat and screamed and started to cry. I swerved into incoming traffic and was lucky enough to get back in my own lane.

What I'm suggesting to City Council is we seriously take a look at some ways to really control this deer population, maybe with a controlled hunt or something like that."

Ask yourself about those two examples. One's very direct and I lead with my face. The other one I tell a story to convince. Which one's a more convincing presentation of a prescription to a broader audience?

What we say, and the order of what we say, is critical.

The next thing is how we say it. Read these sentences aloud. I never said he stole the money. *I* never said he stole the money. I never said *he* stole the money. I never said he stole the *money*.

Each sentence uses the same words but means something different depending on how those words are emphasized. Sometimes it's not what you say, but how you say it. As salespeople, we have to be aware of that.

During this whole part of the presentation, a good salesperson is starting to recognize buying and warning signals or objections. And this is going to lead us into the next phase: dialogue. Those buying signals are anything the buyer says or does, or doesn't say or do, that indicate that they might be interested. These could be things like body language or questions. Even things like, "Tell me more about this, expand on this," from the buyer.

Salespeople need to be hyper-observant. A buyer could be sitting right across from me, nodding and yessing away, but I need to ask: Is this person really interested, or is he just a fantastic listener with great people skills? When the buyer rubs his chin, is he contemplating what I'm saying, or did he suddenly realize he needs a shave?

Our job isn't to read minds, but to be able to determine how interested or not somebody is. Still, we need to tread carefully in our assessment, because we have a tendency in sales to have what's called *attribution bias.* We look for those contributing factors that would cause bias to what we're selling, and ultimately ignore reality.

Chip Heath said it best in *Switch: How to Change Things When Change Is Hard*: "The error lies in our inclination to attribute people's behavior to the way they are, rather than to the situation they are in."

Up until about the last two years, I've been a crazed techie. I'm not very technical, but anytime a new iPhone or something new and innovative has come out, I would immediately get it, regardless of whether I needed it. So much changed in two years that I'm not interested in that now. I'm like that with other things, but there was a time when I would convince myself of all the reasons I needed that new iPhone: This camera's better. It's going to be faster. I'm going to have more access here, here, and here. It didn't matter if I was in contract, I would still need a new iPhone because I looked for contributing factors that would cause my bias.

Salespeople do the same thing. They don't like to see warning signals, challenge them, or get somebody to define a buying signal. They just want to set up in a way that they're going to get a deal. But in reality, anytime anybody makes a decision on anything, what do they do? They ultimately create a pros and cons list, and weigh out all the reasons for versus all the reasons against.

Salespeople are blind a lot of times because they want to sell so bad. They get kind of selfish, maybe a little greedy. They don't want to hear the other side. And that causes them to lose high ground when they get to the closing stage.

That's why the way we look, the order in which we say things, how we say things, and how we act, are all critical in convincing the buyer at the prescription stage that we're somebody to do business with.

Once they decide that, we can enter into dialogue with them.

- You can't value what you can't compare and contrast.

- People justify logically and buy emotionally.

- Less evidence, less chance to sell. More evidence increases your odds.

- In sales, who says so besides you?

- Be fired with enthusiasm ... or you'll be fired with enthusiasm.

CHAPTER EIGHT
Dialogue: Objections Lead to Opportunities

LANCE-ISM #36
"UNCOMFORTABLE CONVERSATIONS ARE THE BEST CONVERSATIONS."

Have you ever heard the story of how McIlhenny's Tabasco sauce got started? I first became familiar with it back when I was an Ivy Leaguer at Dartmouth. Okay, maybe that's a bit of a stretch. I actually dated a young woman who went to Dartmouth, and because she was in her sophomore year, she had to stay at school during the summer. When I went to visit her, I ended up staying all summer, living there and getting a job. So I'd say, technically, that makes me an Ivy Leaguer to some degree.

I ended up hanging with a couple of guys there, you know, fellow Ivy Leaguers. They were from the fraternity that the flick *Animal House* was based on, just to give you some perspective. Every

Wednesday morning at 5 a.m., they'd get up with the sun and do Prairie Fires—a little Tabasco sauce and tequila.

Now if you've ever noticed, a Tabasco bottle has kind of an interesting shape. It actually has a lip on it. Before the Civil War, the McIlhenny family lived on an island along the coast of Louisiana called Avery Island. So if you look at the bottle, you'll see a picture of Avery Island, right there off the coast. The island was just a great place to live—it had sugar cane on it, fresh water, cattle—and the McIlhenny family loved it there.

When the Civil War broke out, some troops were stationed on the island, and they ended up killing the cattle, burning the sugar cane, polluting the water, and further devastating the island. After the Civil War was over, the McIlhenny family had a dilemma. The way they had always lived and made a living was gone. So they sat down, assessed their situation, and essentially asked themselves what they had left. Before long they realized that they had a lot of old bottles still lying around from before the war, these little French perfume bottles, some salt, and a bunch of red-hot Mexican chili peppers. So they decided to go back to an old family recipe and developed the concept of Tabasco. Out of the greatest obstacles, sometimes the best opportunities come about. And now you find Tabasco in most fine restaurants, probably in every supermarket in the country, if not the world, and it's an extremely well known brand.

In every single sale, be it complex or simple, there comes a time where you're going to have to have a dialogue—find out where the buyer's head is. Are they in or out? What do they like or dislike? Many times we hear things that make us think a sale's going pretty well, we feel momentum gaining. And then, all of a sudden, brake lights. Everything comes to a screeching halt. A prospect will say to us: Your price is too high. It's not in the budget. I'm not sure about cost. I'm not sure if your product or solution really has value in my situation. Just like the McIlhenny family, our job is to take objections and conflict and get the buyer to see opportunity.

SPEAKING THE SAME LANGUAGE

Cost. Value. Budget. Price. All those words mean very different things. And in a complex or simple sale, we need to really understand that if we put a definition to all those marketplace-driven objections, what's the difference in those words? Well, we know that those words, those obstacles, all seem like they're the same thing, but they're very different animals. And the first thing we need to do is dig in and really understand the difference.

Ask yourself: What is price? A lot of people say price is defined as the cost of somebody doing something. Fair enough. Sounds logical. The question then becomes: If price is the cost of doing something, then what is cost? It's the price. See what I mean? Those words are used interchangeably, but they're not the same thing.

So let's define price as what the market will bear to pay for a good or service. Take Amazon for instance. They post a price, that's the price. If people buy it, then that's the price. That's evidence of what the market will bear.

Now if somebody says that the cost is too high, do they actually mean cost, or do they mean price? Let's define the word cost. Cost is, for instance, what goes along with a product or service because of ownership. So if I pay a certain price for a home, my costs are things like maintenance. I have to pay for my water, sewer, and electric. They're all costs associated with having a home. If I buy a car, the tires are a cost. Maintenance is a cost. Insurance is a cost.

Price and cost are clearly two different things. But the marketplace uses those words interchangeably. We need to define what they mean to be able to engage in a dialogue about an objection.

Another objection that comes up in more complex sales is: it's not in the budget. The questions you need to ask yourself at that point is: Is budget a number? Do they mean a number? Well, budget means a lot of things. Budget means a time frame, the past performance that dictates future spending. Or do they mean the price is too high? Do they really mean budget? So you might need to educate your prospect to clear up the objection.

If somebody says, "I don't see the value," that's a whole different story. The budget objection seems legitimate. The budget objection seems like it's hard to defend unless you get them to define what it is. But now the objection is about value. What we know about value is it's defined as it's perceived—the eye of the beholder. People can't value what they can't compare and contrast.

IT'S AS EASY AS DDE

So if we look at money objections or financial objections, which many times are the toughest objections to deal with, it's our job as a sales professionals to get the prospect to define, defend, and explain: DDE.

Define, defend, and explain: DDE.

One time we were doing business with an NHL team who was trying to sell a sponsorship package to small- and mid-sized furniture stores around Columbus, Ohio. The package was pretty complex, as they were trying to sell a digital footprint to this furniture store with four locations. They were trying to sell in-game signage, which would drive some traffic to this organization's website, as well as other media—some radio and TV. And they were also trying to sell a little hospitality, a visit from one of the players to come to store openings, and the grand re-opening.

The whole package was well over a quarter-million-dollars, so the stakes were high. The salesperson was doing great. He had the high ground and kicked out a textbook closing question.

"So what are your thoughts on moving forward?" he asked.

"I'm really concerned about the value here," replied the president of the retail store.

So what did the salesperson do? Instead of engaging in DDE at that point, the salesperson took the comment on value at face value, and didn't ask him to define, defend, or explain his position. He went back to the drawing board to carve out some things, trying to hone down, re-propose, and modify the package at a lower price.

When he came back a week later, the salesperson had taken out some of the signage, reduced some of the media spend, trimmed off some of the digital, offered a little less of the hospitality spend, and completely took out the visit from the player to the stores.

What was the president's response? "I'm really not interested at this point."

In time the salesperson was able to re-engage the buyer. One day he approached him and just laid it out there.

"What happened?" asked the salesman. "You said you didn't see value in what we were offering, so we got the price down."

"Yeah, the spending was a little higher than we wanted," agreed the president of the company. "But when you came back with the package, you actually took out the thing that was most valuable to me."

"What was that?" asked the salesman.

"The player visit."

It was then that the salesperson realized that he didn't ask the buyer to force-rank which things were most important. He actually took out the thing that was *least* expensive for the team, which was the easiest thing for them to do as it held the least value on their end.

But the buyer had ranked the player visit as the highest value. That knee-jerk move devalued the whole deal.

So it's our job as salespeople to really get a clear understanding of what the buyer is saying. And chances are if you look at marketplace-driven objections, everybody defines those words very differently, and uses them interchangeably. We are obligated as salespeople to have a dialogue about what those objections are, not to make assumptions.

Then there are inherent objections that go even deeper.

Buyers are incessantly preoccupied, and they become disinterested. So we need to address preoccupation at all times during the sales process. We've got to engage disinterest. They'll doubt what we say, which we must counter with evidence. Of course, there are constants like procrastination, stalls, and indecision.

Then there's another layer of objections: perception, credibility, bias. There are even half-baked objections because people haven't thought things through. We have to deal with all of these at different times in the sales process, but no more importantly than after we prescribe a solution.

We've got to create a dialogue that causes that buyer to feel comfortable talking to us, to be candid with us. Our questioning needs to be fantastic. If they're not candid and giving us a half-baked objection, it's because they haven't thought through our solution.

We have to have the right strategy when dealing with objection in the dialogue stage. We need to clarify the objection, find points of agreement, and then we have to create a compelling prescription to move forward.

At this point in the sales process, we have a choice as a salesperson, and a lot of salespeople fail this test. Many have the ability to start negotiating/bargaining. And this is where a lot of salespeople start because they don't read the situation right, and they really don't get the buyer to define the objection. They start reacting instead of responding and being proactive. And the lowest ground we can take as a salesperson is being reactive.

The lowest ground we can take as a salesperson is being reactive.

Like in my example with the NHL sales rep, oftentimes once a salesperson hears any kind of objection, especially regarding financial, they start to throw better deals at the buyer before they get the buyer to defend and define the objection. You can't bargain if you're blind. Yet that's what a lot of salespeople do. They start to invoke the negotiation process before they've defined the objection, or made the buyer defend the objection. They address the objection as soon as they hear it, they react to it, and they end up playing the game of whack-a-mole.

When you buy anything in life, you have reasons for it and reasons against it. There are logical reasons to justify the buy and there are emotional reasons that will help you justify the buy. Some people buy things because they can. Some people buy things because they need to. Some people do things out of abundance, others out of scarcity. The words negotiation and objection are just like the word pornography.

Most people can describe what negotiating and objection is, but they are hard to define because they are so subjective. The reason why I say it's like pornography is because in the 1964 court case of *Jacobellis v. Ohio*, U.S. Supreme Court justice Potter Stewart wrote that "hard-core pornography" was hard to define, but that "I know it when I see it.[13] Keeping this definition in mind, there are people who say Michelangelo's *David* is pornography.

Have you heard the one about the patient going in to see his therapist about sex-related issues? The patient sits down on the

---

13   "Potter Stewart," Wikipedia, last modified May 9, 2018, https://en.wikipedia.org/wiki/Potter_Stewart.

couch, and the therapist brings out a stack of inkblots. He shows the first inkblot to the patient.

"What do you see here?"

"Sex," says the patient.

The doctor makes a note, then whips out another ink blot.

"How about this one?"

"Sex," says the patient again.

The doctor makes another note, then shuffles out another inkblot.

"What about this one?"

"Sex," says the patient.

By now the doctor is stumped, so he looks at the inkblot, but sees a butterfly. He shrugs and begins firing off one inkblot after another.

"Sex. Sex. Sex," says the patient over and over.

The doctor looks at the patient sternly. "Stop saying everything reminds you of sex!"

The patient leaps to his feet. "Well, stop showing me dirty pictures!"

So, when we hear an objection and when we negotiate in the dialogue stage, we really need to think about those words. Let's define an objection as an obstacle. And let's say negotiate is synonymous with navigate. I could navigate my car around obstacles into a parking space. I navigate my boat carefully around a series of obstacles into a dock or a slip. So, negotiation and objection go hand in hand. We negotiate around objections, and we navigate a conversation. That's dialogue.

NEVER DO BATTLE WITH THE BUYER

If you look at any negotiation process, there's a lot of wording out there about battling an objection. If I'm trying to do business with you, I don't know if we're necessarily going to do battle. I think the wiser choice is to first find out where we agree. I've watched a lot of high-level negotiators in my life. We watch a lot of sponsorships and naming-rights deals being done with stadiums, and were actually able to buck some of the largest naming rights. I've never seen high-level lawyers and salespeople battle. Our observations are that they find points of agreement. When Eric Sudol is negotiating the naming rights for AT&T Stadium, I don't see him necessarily battling with AT&T. I think they're finding points of agreement. Even when watching the Cleveland Browns come up with a beer deal for their stadium at FirstEnergy Stadium with Anheuser-Busch. I don't see them battling with Anheuser-Busch; I think there's a lot of positioning that goes on. It's not a battle, because if we're going to try to ultimately do business with each other for a long period of time, battling doesn't do anybody justice.

We actually have to find points of agreement. This is because we're trying to overcome a preoccupation of someone being indecisive, and we need to create a compelling reason or story to move ahead. If there's not a compelling reason to move ahead, nobody's going to move ahead.

We don't deal with objections; we deal with people. We resolve objections.

We don't deal with objections; we deal with people. We resolve objections.

The first thing we do is a visual. We need to create visuals to remind the buyer of their need or want.

As when we discussed the hotel example, we attacked the issue with: "You're really looking to save these carpets a little longer, right?"

(1) Remind them of their need.

"Would you agree that with some of the seating solutions we put in front of you, you'd be able to do that?"

(2) Remind them that your product or service can actually address that want, need, or gap.

"So, just making sure we're on the same page: what you're looking to do is give a thousand guests in this double-banquet hall here a great time, along with some chairs that endure a lot of ups and downs and being pulled in and out. What you'll want to see after having this place filled with guests for three months in a row, is that there's very little wear and tear in your busy season, as well as want stellar reports back from your maintenance, is that right?"

(3) Paint that word picture.

I need to be able to use these visuals to make sure I'm on the same page with the buyer. That's gaining the high ground.

A buyer might come off and answer, "Yeah, but I'm still concerned about price," or, "I'm still concerned about whether this system's gonna work."

Now I'm starting to root out very specific things that people are going to object to. And in the moment, many times salespeople just don't do a good job. For instance, if you were selling software and you positioned everything perfectly, used your facts and benefits, nailed that visual and said, "So, what are your thoughts on those reports?"

Yet the buyer still comes back with: "You know, I'm still concerned about the pricing of this and the timing." You have to be able to, in the moment, accept that and root out the objection. Don't swim away from it like it's a turd in a pool. Is it legit or not? Salespeople need to be really good at cushioning, because you have to be able to categorize that objection. Is that a put off? Is that genuine? Is that a misconception? Are you giving me something that is biased, or is that something that is half-baked?

When it comes to objections, the absolute lowest ground a salesperson can take is to deal with it in the moment.

So what's the highest ground? To deal with an objection before it actually ever comes up.

The second highest ground for a salesperson to take is to bring up objections

Deal with an objection before it actually ever comes up.

themselves: What are some of your concerns? What are some things you don't like about what we presented to you? What are some things you do like?

When it comes to an objection, we need to resolve them whether they are voiced or not. We need to at least ask for them. And chances are we've dealt with the objection a little bit before it came out, because most salespeople get the same objection in different incarnations. Believe it or not, there are only so many kinds of objections salespeople get. Don't agree or disagree with the objection. Acknowledge. Then ask another question to clarify.

"So tell me a little bit more about it, give me an example."

Force it back on the buyer to paint the picture. Then ask another question: "What else besides that is causing you to hesitate?"

Chances are, probably nothing.

"Well, if we can address that, would you at least be willing to move forward?"

At this point you've corralled the buyer into a yes or no.

Or they might say: "No, I didn't say that," which would prompt: "Geez, sounds like there's something else causing your hesitation."

You need to have a questioning model that clarifies objections so you're not playing whack-a-mole. And there's always a chance that you might not be able to resolve an objection. But after you know where they stand, you have to decide what kind of evidence or other assistance you need. Maybe you need to bargain a little bit, go deeper, or get more evidence. Remember, the objective is to move to the close stage.

DON'T SETTLE FOR MAYBE

The overarching goal is to cause the buyer to say *something*. I've got to cause him or her to say yes, no, or maybe.

And for the record, maybes suck.

Way back in eighth grade, I had a bit of a ballsy moment. I had my eye on this girl in class, and I needed an angle. What did I do? I decided to toss the choice in her court. I passed her a note, "Will you go to the dance with me?" with the following three options:

Now, in this situation, as a fourteen-year-old boy, you want the yes. The no is bad for your self-esteem. But the maybe gives you hope.

We'll get to what the girl said in a minute, but for now, let's talk about how this same situation is a problem in sales.

In short: we have too many maybe answers.

This biggest challenge in B2B selling today is best explained by how every salesperson should conceptualize a pipeline. In general:

33% of our pipeline will buy from us in the near future.

33% of our pipeline will buy in the far future.

33% will never buy from us—even if we tried to sell them something worth $1 for ninety cents.

Sometimes I call sales reps "Prisoners of Hope," because they don't ask for the order. In sales, a Prisoner of Hope is someone who continues to accept the maybe. They spend too much time misinterpreting buying and warning signals, so sales cycles are too long, or they carry on forever and then just die out in the end.

We've all seen these situations, or even been in them. It always looks like this:

"I don't want to talk right now. But in three months, we can talk …"

"We need a lot of internal stakeholders to agree before we can commit …"

"Send me your materials and I'll take a look …"

A buyer acts very interested and then goes phantom on us. And, to try and make the sale or get context, we resort to stalking, creeping, doing fly-bys on social media, or calling from unlisted numbers.

Ultimately, our prospects are being nice. They feel bad about saying no, so they don't. They string us along. But here's the deal: we can't change them. The only person we can change is ourselves.

Go back to these bullets right above here. See how they end with ellipses? It's all people trailing off. That usually means "no" in reality, but the trail-off implies some hope for the sales rep. You become a Prisoner of Hope and here's what happens: your prospects stay in the pipeline for way too long, and they almost never close. 90 percent or more of these Prisoner of Hope situations go nowhere.

All these leads are circling Maybe on your eighth grade note pass. You've got hope, but you've got no dance card. However you cut it, it's not the best approach in terms of sales tactics.

Asking for the order is the beginning phase of getting an objection. You need the objection (the "no") in order to move to the next step. Conflict drives everything, and that's especially true in sales.

Here are three quick tips:

1. **Be in the moment.** I like scripts and call flows as much as the next guy, and I've trained people on scripts and working with checklists and boxes to hit. It's all well and good. But people with purchasing authority in organizations are usually seasoned. They've been around the block and they know the tactics and angles too. They're going to respond more to a real conversation with ups and downs, sidebars, small talk, and commonalities than being sold from a script. The moment changes. Example: You go in and you want to sell a season ticket package. You've got a whole plan of sales tactics to get there. Minutes into this interaction, the guy wants to talk about his vacation to Mo'orea. You've never been to Mo'orea, and have no idea where it is. So what now? You get in the moment. Listen to him, or maybe Google a few things about Mo'orea. Talk about how you want to go now, too. It's read and react. You can go in with a baseline, but what happens in the moment matters.

2. **Ask good closing questions.** There are a million studies about the power of asking good questions. You need to get to them to make the close. In general, yes/no questions don't get you as far. If the target is busy, yes/no can detach them from the sales process, because they're just giving you quick, one-word answers. Make them think. They need to be talking about their pain points and what your solution is going to do for that problem. Remember, some products are sold because they are needed, and some are sold as an opportunity.

3. **Don't be afraid to ask.** We all know people like this, and confidence varies. But that's part of the Prisoner of Hope

problem. Jump over the confidence hurdle and ask. It's the only way to receive. What's the worst that happens? If they say no, there's the conflict! You can drive forward from there.

This is my baseline approach to the sales strategy of the power of no, and using conflict to drive forward. We need to get to high ground and shut down the idea of artificial harmony quickly. Use conflict to drive sales forward and get to the close.

By the way, the girl said *maybe*.

- They sell hearing aids, not listening aids. Start hearing what your prospect is saying.

- Objections are when the real selling starts.

- Everyone wants to feel that they got a good deal.

- You can't bargain if you're blind. Negotiation is navigation.

- The best time to deal with an objection is before it comes up. That's **high** ground. The worst time to deal with an objection is in the moment. That's **low** ground.

CHAPTER NINE
Close: Prepare for Landing

LANCE-ISM #108
"COFFEE IS FOR CLOSERS."

There's a famous sales study from the 1970s, done by Mutual of Omaha. The set-up is this: they went to their home market (Omaha) and targeted some folks who would be good customers for them. They picked about 1,000 people and said they'd give them insurance premiums (up to $500,000) for a year, but they had to meet with Mutual's salespeople in order to get this offer. At the same time, they told 150 sales people that there were 1,000 available leads. The whole transaction was contingent on the salespeople asking a specific closing question. Unless that question was asked, nothing was triggered. There was no close.

So, out of these 1,000 really good, vetted leads, what percentage do you think closed?

It was about 7 percent. About seventy out of 1,000 people. And why? Because the salespeople weren't asking the question. They left about 930 leads on the table because they didn't ask.

The fact is, there's no skill in closing. Real closers are like fairies, pixies, and leprechauns. They just don't exist. However, if you ever looked at the classifieds in a magazine or online for sales jobs, companies are always looking to hire closers. It's become kind of a mystical thing that the skill is really in closing.

I travel fifty times a year, and I don't know a ton about flight or being a pilot, but this is kind of my thought process: there's a lot to take into consideration when a plane's taking off. You have to have enough thrust, enough fuel, you've got to think of headwinds, and be able to get to the right speed to get that plane to take off. And I always think that the skill set with a plane is really about getting it up in the air. I fly enough that it still amazes me that a two-ton piece of steel tubing can thrust itself through the air at hundreds of miles an hour and stay in the air. I'm not afraid of flying, by the way. If anything, I'm afraid of crashing.

When I think about flying though, and mind you I'm not a very scientific man, I think about gravity. I know at some point, intentionally or not, that plane's going to come down. Gravity is going to pull it down. And I think with the assistance of gravity, ultimately to close the deal, the plane's going to come down. You're going to bring it down for a landing.

I liken that process, where the majority of the heavy lifting is done in the beginning, to sales. I think at some level, like I've discussed, sales is nothing more than an algorithm—a series of yesses. And most of the time the challenge with closing comes with inherent objections.

It's kind of like Friday night at our house, when I ask my wife if she wants to go out to dinner.

She'll say, "yeah."

And then I say, "Where do you want to go?"

She'll say, "I don't know. Where do you want to go?"

I'll make some suggestions, and she'll say something like, "I'm not sure," or "No, I don't like that."

There's a lot of indecision in every decision. And what we're dealing with at the end of most sales processes, whether we're closing something major or something relatively minor, there's indecision. But there's really not a lot of skill in moving past that point. My wife and I either starve to death, or we figure it out.

THE SKILL OF CLOSING

There's actually zero skill in closing. The sale has to come to a freaking end. It might not roll in your favor, you might not get the deal, or you might get a no. You certainly don't want a maybe because maybes suck, as I found out in the eighth grade.

Recently, I was on the phone with my VP of sales, Allison, and we were talking to Dave and Buster's. Allison said, "Hey, I haven't been on call with you for a while. Would you give me some feedback?"

I said, "certainly." So before long we were pitching this big VP from Dave and Buster's, named Jackie.

At the end, Allison was asking good questions. "So what are your thoughts moving forward?"

Jackie laid out how to follow up and said, "Give me a couple weeks. Let's talk then."

"That's great," replied Allison. "So we'll kind of target the next two weeks."

I stopped because I was waiting for Allison to say something, and she didn't. That's when I sprung into action.

"Hey, Jackie," I said. "You're so busy. Why don't we pencil in Monday the ninth? Say, one o'clock, so you're not chasing us; we're not chasing you. We just have it locked in, and we'll discuss whether we move forward with this pilot or not."

"That's fine," she said.

We got off the phone and Allison said, "You have some feedback?"

"Your opening was rock solid. I probably would have had her give her observations first. Remember, telling's not selling. And then the other thing is that you left the next steps open. You were way too casual with it."

"What do you mean?" she asks.

"You were just going to leave it at, 'Hey, let's follow up in a couple weeks.' And it was going so well, Allison," I said. "I get why you were doing that. But sales is all about artificial momentum. *You* have to create next steps, close, and create decisiveness. So, you're dealing with indecisiveness; you need decisive, right? In Latin, that means to cut off from. You cut off other possibilities; you slice. And I know that sounds kind of crude or whatever, but that's what you're doing. That's why you need a yes or no; that's why maybe sucks. So even in that spot, even though that was an incremental agreement to move forward, you had a next step locked in. See, if you didn't have that locked in, it's easier for her to put you off longer and not do business with you."

VARIANTS OF CLOSING

So, closing's not a skill. It's just a matter of landing the airplane. It's advancing things to the next steps, asking if somebody is in or out. The easiest way to close a deal is the Nike close: just do it.

We watch a lot of industries. We're not really into the Cheesy Close. The hardest thing to do sometimes is ask for money. We watch some industries, especially in pro sports, we'll say, "Hey, you want to put this on your American Express Black Card?" Sometimes you're just awkward asking for money. That's a Nike close. Let's do this; let's sign here. You stick the contract in front of them, and you need to be ready when you close, because you may have to go back into the dialogue piece and deal with objections.

Sometimes when you close, you have another round of objections or negotiating. About a year ago we bought a copier, and one of the salespeople asked me early on, "What's your budget?"

I just looked at him. "What my budget is for this copier, since we don't need one, is half your best offer."

He starts laughing.

"No, seriously," I said. "Maybe we can trade this copier out for something like sales training. That's a horrible question. Nobody is ever going to give their budget to you."

Now, we ended up buying the copier, but near the end of the sale he said, "So, how do you feel about the copier?"

That's not a great closing question. Why? Because he doesn't really care, and doesn't really want to know how I feel about the copier.

"Is the price good? Let's move forward."

I said, "The price is great."

"Okay, let's sign here."

I said, "Whoa, whoa, whoa. We talked about the price, but we haven't talked about terms." In the close, you might actually have to deal with another round where you get into formal negotiations. Or you might head back into the dialogue stage again, where you're negotiating or dealing with objections.

You can go for an Alternate Choice Close as well: Do you want option A or B? Do you want to go with the three-year contract or the seven-year contract? Do you want this section or that section?

But that ends up being more of a Trial Close as opposed to a Direct Close.

But as you can see, there's really no skill in this. They're not deep questions. You're bringing the plane down for a landing.

Variants of Closings

 Direct Close   (4) Next Step Close

 Alternate Choice Close   (5) Opportunity Close

(3) Minor Point Close   (6) Balancing Close

Though the Direct Close is always preferred, you could go with a Minor Point Close, depending on the situation.

When I first bought club seats at the Cleveland Cavaliers, a guy, named Bob Sivik, was selling me the club seats. They were going for about $20,000 per year; you get four club seats, all food inclusive, you get to watch Cavs and LeBron.

Bob started with: "So what are your thoughts on moving forward?"

I said, "Well, I gotta think about this."

Then he Minor-Pointed me. "Well, do you want the names on the seats in your name or your company's name?"

I looked at Bob. "What do you mean?"

"Well, there's a little placard in these seats in the club level, and they could actually have your personal name or your company's."

"Well, I'd want my company's name."

He had me. What he was doing with that Minor Close was gauging my interest.

There's also a Next Step Close. A lot of times when we are setting up a training, we may be at a hotel doing an on-site meeting, and the hotel rep might say something like, "What are your thoughts on this?" And they'll actually show us a room, thinking beyond the close to the next step.

Then there's one that a lot of organizations use. It's called the Opportunity Close. Or I call it the K-Mart shopper close: "Hey, K-Mart shoppers. Charmin toilet paper is on sale. In aisle seven for the next forty-five minutes, you can pick up a four pack for just forty-nine cents a roll."

Often, organizations will pressure the buyer by giving them a time frame, or telling them if they act now, they will get a discount. Infomercials and timeshares are notorious for this kind of close. Our suggestion here is never to lead with this one, because it's the most manipulative close that can be used. We're not saying not to use it. We would lead with the Direct Close.

I once had somebody from the Philadelphia Chamber of Commerce call me. We belonged to another chamber at the time, and she asked why we belonged to one chamber versus the other.

She had this great pitch. But I just came back, and said, "Listen, as much as we benefit by belonging to this other chamber, our health insurance is positively affected. That's all it really comes down to. Actually, doing business with you guys here at the Philly Chamber would be probably a little better with all the incentives you have. Essentially, though, if you can show me that I can get my health insurance like I do now through this other chamber, we'd definitely consider it."

So she comes back to me a couple days later and said, "Can we do this?"

It was around June at that time. I said, "Listen, we're in. Our membership with this other chamber ends in December. We're just not going to belong to two chambers at once, but I'll send a letter, give my commitment, blah-blah-blah."

She was really cool about it. She came back in July. "Hey, I want to let you know that our chamber here starts August first."

She came back again in August. "Our chamber starts September first. I just had to let you know our membership fees are going up, and I really think you should take advantage of this."

"That's very thoughtful," I said. "I really appreciate you thinking of me. We're absolutely in. We're just not going to belong to two chambers at once. It's not responsible. We're a small organization."

She pushed back. "Lance, I really think this is a good deal."

I said, "I do appreciate you thinking of me. I'm going to politely decline. We're in the other chamber."

She came back a third time, but this time really hard. I said, "Look, Lara. You open for some coaching?"

"Yeah."

"Well, number one, I never gave you the price objection. The only thing I said was we shouldn't belong to two chambers at once. I said we're in. You said we could do it. We're going to do it. It's better we belong here. I just don't want two at once."

She whacks me again with it: "I just think it's a great deal."

"Whoa." I said. "Stop. Now I'm kind of pissed off. What makes you think I won't get this discount later."

"Well, you won't," she said.

"Now that you're challenging me, oh, trust me, I *will* get the discount when I sign up. Whether or not you get the deal, it'll be completely up to how hard you push me one more time. But I will get the rates in December that you're pitching me now."

"I don't think you will."

"Well, I probably won't be going through you, but I will call the chamber directly."

The end of the story? I ended up getting the rates that I wanted. But the point is she just came in too hard with that Opportunity Close. Because the fact is, not everybody objects to money. My objection wasn't about money. It was about logistics.

So then the last close is more of a weighing things, or what we call a Balancing Close. That close is right out of Ben Franklin's playbook, in fact. I can't overstate that, next to this one, the best sales book you'll ever read is Ben Franklin's autobiography. He's really the only American philosopher we had. And he's one of our only inventors *and* philosophers.

And how did Ben Franklin make decisions? Ultimately weighing things. He basically made decisions from a pro/con standpoint, so any major business decision he got into or anything he was trying to do, he'd make a list, do a t-chart, and say: here are the pros and cons.

If the cons weighed out the pros, he wouldn't do it. If the pros weighed out the cons, he would do it. Well, there's something to be said about that in sales, because in sales, most decisions that are made are weighed or balanced against each other. When I bought my pair of sneakers, I weighed: should I have them as opposed to not have them?

As salespeople, that's one of our tools to take the high ground, and to really help somebody go backwards through the process and weigh options against one another. This works with selling to buying groups. This works when selling to individuals. Because that's exactly how they're going to make a decision.

We call it the Balance Close or the Weighing Close because essentially you could have seven feathers against and three rocks for. Which would weigh more? It's not necessarily the quantity of pros or cons, but the quality. The rocks would weigh more and win. But that's a move, and salespeople forget that.

Remember, closing is all based off the momentum you built up until that point, and just like with the plane, it's going to land. How smooth it lands is all a matter of how well you did in directing it toward the runway.

- There's no skill in closing!
- Don't be afraid of flying, be afraid of crashing. The plane has to come down. Close the sale.
- When closing, be careful of being cheesy.
- There's more than one way to close.
- Read Ben Franklin.

CONCLUSION

CONGRATULATIONS! YOU'VE REACHED THE END ZONE!

The good news is that we've found the enemy. The bad news is that it's you. You're the only person in the whole world who can change yourself. Is that easy or hard? Definitely hard. It's so hard, in fact, that we spend all our time trying to change everybody else instead.

Let me leave you with a poem:

The task is to build a better world;
I answered: "How?
The world is so large vast and complicated now,
and I, so small and useless, there's nothing I can do."
My dad in all his wisdom said,
"Lance, just build a better you."

Hopefully this book will help you build a better you.
Good luck! And happy selling!

ACKNOWLEDGMENTS

Selling may be an away game, but writing this book has been a roadshow. It's been built on the backs of hard work, sweat, and debate from a lot of people.

Thanks to my mom and dad for always pushing me to go out on my own and start my own company. Both served as a good example and reminder to take risks and seize opportunities. It's easy to take on an endeavor like this when you have such a solid home front. Thanks to my brothers—never forget how we were raised with arguments, disagreements, and love. You have to pound the impurities out of iron to make it stronger which is exactly what we did. It made us all better. Thanks to my three sons who are constantly striving to get to the next level. They are always my motivation. Thanks to Lisa, who is always my steady rock and keeps my priorities right in front of me. My friend, Rick Slatowski, I'll always remember our good times. Mike Borusiewicz, thanks for handing me my first Dale Carnegie book to get started. Your desire to always improve yourself is something I will never forget.

Thanks to Mark Norman who took a gamble and hired me at Dale Carnegie. He taught me how to sell and do public speaking. Thanks to Sam Iorio who taught me how to be a sales leader, made a good businessman out of me, and gave me a shot to own my own business. Thanks to Ed Eppley who was a great business partner, coach, and Lance whisperer in growing our business our way (Death to the Empire). Thanks to the original soup club: Chad Estis and Mike Ondrejko. I loved how we solved the world's business issues over a bowl of soup. To all the crews at the Browns, Legends, and Cowboys, thanks for all of the intense coaching and training sessions. You all have pushed me as much as I have pushed you.

Traci Tigue, Allison Schuller, Larry Prevost, and Lauren Snyder, your loyalty, hard work, and dedication has always made this fun and has allowed this book to be written alongside our growing business. Jessica Eickholt, you have been with me through three different companies and you are, without doubt, a trusted advisor. Sian Valentine, we have worked together for so long. Your hard work and dedication has allowed me to accomplish so much. Not only are you my right hand, but my left as well. Desireé Hoffman, thanks for pushing, persevering, and making sure all the t's are crossed and the i's are dotted. Your advice and coaching are always welcomed.

ABOUT THE AUTHOR

Over the past two decades, Lance Tyson has followed his passion for developing strong business leaders and their salespeople by tapping into his natural ability to connect with others and foster an environment for learning and coaching.

As owner, president, and CEO of Tyson Group, Lance facilitates, trains, and conducts over one hundred workshops annually in areas such as performance management, leadership, sales, sales management, customer service, and team building.

In 2002, Lance took over several Dale Carnegie Training operations in the Midwest. He started with Cleveland, then moved on to Columbus, and eventually took over the Cincinnati and Indianapolis marketplaces. Under Lance's leadership, these marketplaces experienced 230 percent growth to become the largest Dale Carnegie Training operation. In 2010, Lance sold his interest in Dale Carnegie and formed PRSPX in Dublin, Ohio to help clients build effective sales ecosystems. PRSPX has since been restructured as Tyson Group in order to provide services to assess sales teams, diagnose their needs, and equip them to be better salespeople and leaders. Lance now focuses on the mission of Tyson Group: to coach, train, and consult with sales leaders and their teams to compete in a complex world.

Lance currently lives in Dublin, Ohio with his wife and three kids.